ROGUE TRIDENT

ROGUE TRIDENT

by
JOHN R. HINDINGER

authorHOUSE™

1663 LIBERTY DRIVE, SUITE 200
BLOOMINGTON, INDIANA 47403
(800) 839-8640
WWW.AUTHORHOUSE.COM

First published by AuthorHouse 08/22/05

ISBN: 1-4140-6395-4 (e)
ISBN: 1-4184-3250-4 (sc)
ISBN: 1-4184-3249-0 (dj)

Printed in the United States of America
Bloomington, Indiana

This book is printed on acid-free paper.

I dedicate this story to

My parents - John and Helen Hindinger
My best friend - Christine Behnken
My mentors - Jerry Gross and Bill Linn
My brothers — every sailor who served with pride beneath the waves

CHAPTER ONE

DAVID BASS, A STOCKY MAN in his early twenties, sat before the reactor panel, a sprawling table of controls and gauges that climbed up the forward wall of the engine room's maneuvering control center.

Beside him, a junior electrician named Dowd bit his nails while glancing at displays that resembled the reactor panel but instead routed electric power. To Bass' other side stood the steam panel that controlled vapor flow to the submarine's twin main engines.

Bass heard Lieutenant Jake Slate's voice crackle through the wireless unit at his hip.

"This is the duty officer," Jake said. "Report shore power load."

Bass glanced over Dowd's shoulder at gauges on the electric panel.

"Nine hundred amps aft, eight hundred forward, sir."

Bass reached behind his shoulder for the engine room announcing circuit. He pulled the handset to his mouth, clicked it, and paused. The microphone click signaled his accomplice to join him in maneuvering.

"What's wrong? Cat got your tongue?" Dowd asked.

"I was going to ask Gant to run forward and get me a Coke, but then I remembered that the crew's mess is not a happy place right now."

"No kidding! Running a security drill the night before patrol is a bunch of crap. Everyone is just trying to get some sleep. I can't believe Mister Slate would do that."

Bass pretended to listen as Michael Gant, a lumpy, bucktoothed Tennessee native in his mid-twenties, snuck up to maneuvering's open entryway and struck Dowd's head with a three-foot torque wrench.

Dowd recoiled onto the electric panel. He staggered to his feet and pressed his palm against his wound. Bass punched him in the stomach as Gant crashed the wrench down again. Dowd fell to the floor.

While Gant mummified his victim with industrial tape, Bass reached for the electric panel. Trembling hands twisted voltage and amperage control knobs, straining the submarine's battery and reducing the load on shore electricity. Bass returned to the reactor panel and called Jake Slate.

"Sir, we're set down here," he said. "Ready to divorce from shore power and commence a reactor start-up."

"Got it. What about Dowd?" Jake asked.

"He's wrapped up."

"No problems?"

"It's fine. Everything's fine," Bass said.

"Okay, commence a reactor start-up. Have Gant bleed steam around the number two main steam valve and start the port side of the engine room. Cut any corner to get it done."

Paranoid, Bass glanced down the eight-foot wide tunnel, a radiation-shielded passage through the reactor compartment that provided the only path between the engine room and the rest of the USS *Colorado*. No one was coming.

He crossed in front of maneuvering where gray towers of reactor circuitry covered the deck plates. Kneeling between symmetric panels, he slid a toolbox to his knees and flipped open the lid to expose the specialized fuses that operated the reactor's control rods. He unlocked a Plexiglas shield and popped a fuse in a socket, completing a circuit to a motor on top of the reactor.

Gant appeared from behind the corner.

"Bass, I bypassed the port main steam valve," he said. "I need to place the aux steam reducer on line and draw vacuum in the condenser. Then I'm going to place feed and condensate on line. It's going to take me a while by myself, but I'm making good time. How are you doing?"

"Don't worry, dude. We're going to limp out of here on the emergency propulsion motor anyway. We'll have the main engine up before anyone even knows we're gone."

Bass could see the veins in Gant's neck throbbing. He heard tension in his voice.

"I think I killed Dowd. Are we crazy, man?"

"Get over it," Bass said. "He'll be fine. The whole crew is going to be fine. Hell, they ought to thank us for getting them out of the patrol. We take this pig and they get a vacation. And we get ten million each. No more debt and no more Navy."

"What if something goes wrong?"

"It won't. Mister Slate knows what he's doing. This is money in the bank."

Topside, Jake scanned the explosive handling wharf to verify that no one was watching him. Below the pier, two of the six Taiwanese commandos who had just swum to the submarine slinked along a wooden catwalk toward electrical junction boxes.

Jake tugged his ball cap. The Taiwanese swimmers tripped breakers that cut the *Colorado* from shore power and left it to rely on its battery. The commandos slipped into the water and mounted the rounded bow where they unraveled nylon ropes from the submarine's cleats.

Jake shifted his gaze to the stern and saw swimmers unscrewing shore power cables from the *Colorado*'s aft external power connections. He craned his neck the opposite way and studied two more commandos as they removed the forward electric cables.

Pierre Renard, an international arms dealer, and Sergeant Kao Yatsen, a veteran Taiwanese commando, waddled toward Jake in swim fins while balancing the weight of their rebreathers. Panting, Renard seemed uncomfortable with the equipment. Kao appeared older than Renard but moved fluidly.

"Mister Slate," Kao said in accented but confident English, "I am Mister Lion, leader of your commando team. Have you prepared the ship for boarding?"

Renard had informed Jake that the Taiwanese Para-Frogmen at his disposal would guard their identities. Mission names had to supplant real names, and Jake had suggested predatory felines. Given that the Taiwanese culture respected large cats – naming most of its submarines after them – the names fit.

"We're ready," Jake said.

Kao snapped an order in Mandarin. Two men dropped mooring lines and walked toward Kao, their fins slapping the hull with each step.

"The rest will join us after the electric cables are removed," Kao said. "May we begin the insertion?"

"Follow me," Jake said.

Jake descended a ten-foot ladder through a dual hatch into the *Colorado*'s missile compartment. Green lights on parallel gray switchboards indicated that the submarine's battery bore the electrical load. No loss of lighting or equipment had alerted the crew.

Three commandos and the Frenchman surrounded him at the bottom of the ladder. They tossed their fins, rebreathers, and facemasks behind a switchboard.

Jake felt the commandos' eyes on him as he trotted to a metal locker. He reached for a key dangling from a lanyard on his belt and slid it into the *Colorado*'s gun vault. The door creaked open, revealing rifles, pistols, shotguns and ammunition. Commandos encircled the locker.

Jake slid to a nearby workbench. He jammed another key into the bench's top drawer and pulled out a Jacksonville Jaguars gym bag that contained silencers, ski masks, and sunglasses. It also held three pairs of handcuffs he had purchased from a pawn shop.

Jake watched the warriors attach silencers to the barrels of their small arms and prepare rifles for their comrades who remained topside. The eldest commando readied a pistol for Jake.

"The weapon is silenced and loaded with seven rounds. The trigger safety is engaged," Kao said. "Your backup clips hold seven rounds each."

Jake pushed the slide safety of his Beretta to the right with his thumb, arming the weapon. The remaining commandos descended into the missile compartment and grabbed weapons from their comrades.

Six armed commandos, disguised in black, faced him.

"Which ones are Mister Cheetah and Mister Tiger?" Jake asked.

Two frogmen raised fists. The duo represented the insertion team's physical extremes.

Cheetah stood five and a half feet tall. Jake noticed small bumps on his wetsuit that indicated lean muscle underneath.

Wiry guys are scrappy, Jake thought.

Tiger stood over six feet tall, and his shoulders spanned nearly as wide. He stared at Jake with an arrogant smugness.

Shit, he's big, Jake thought.

"Mister Cheetah and Mister Tiger," Jake said, "climb back up the ladder and guard topside. The rest of you put your sunglasses on.

"Mister Renard, go to maneuvering," Jake said. "We already control it. You'll be safe there."

Jake sent Renard, the only other hijacker who could navigate the submarine, to the engine room as insurance in case he took a bullet while taking the *Colorado*.

"You can do this, *mon ami*. I have the utmost confidence in you," Renard said.

"At this point," Jake said, "you have no choice."

Renard left Jake with four commandos.

"Okay. You guys - over there."

Jake pointed, and as commandos hid behind cabinets, he stepped deeper into the missile compartment.

Containing little more than manholes bolted over missile guidance innards, the compartment's upper level was a barren land. Jake expected no company but threw his voice into a forest of missile tubes.

"Rover!" Jake said. "This is the duty officer. Is the rover watch in upper level?"

Relieved by the silence, he snapped a handset from a brass cradle. He telephoned CAMP, the control and monitoring panel, one deck below.

"CAMP," a watchman said.

"CAMP, Duty Officer," Jake said. "Have the rover report to your station. I want to talk to both of you on my way by."

While Jake marched back to Kao's team, he heard the watchman's voice crackle over the missile compartment announcing circuit.

"Rover, come to CAMP."

"The rover should be at CAMP soon," Jake said to the masked commandos. "When I secure the two men there, I'll give the signal."

"In two minutes, we move regardless," Kao said. "There are silencers on these weapons for a reason."

Gym bag in hand, Jake scurried down the staircase to the missile compartment's second level.

Wide orange tubes containing missiles twenty-three and twenty-four stood before him. He stepped around them and passed equipment that controlled the temperature and humidity within each missile's housing.

Near an alcove between towers of electronics, a boot from the CAMP watch, Missile Technician Second Class Joseph Ellen, rested in Jake's path.

"Did the rover acknowledge?" Jake asked.

"Yes, sir," Ellen said. "Here he comes now."

A man with sandy blond hair turned the corner around tube one. Over his bell-bottom trousers, he wore an olive web belt with a forty-five caliber pistol and two clips.

Jake knew that Sonar Technician Second Class Welch was happier sitting in front of the displays in the *Colorado*'s air-conditioned sonar room than marching around the missile compartment. His frown revealed his frustration in being interrupted from his rounds.

"What's up, sir?" Welch asked.

"Not much," Jake said. "I just need you and Ellen to go stand over there."

Jake withdrew his pistol from the gym bag and pointed at a towering electronic cabinet.

"What the fuck?" Welch asked.

Jake pointed the barrel at Welch. He put his free hand into the bag, pulled out a pair of handcuffs, and slid them across the deck.

"Welch, put this around your left wrist," Jake said.

Shaking, Welch picked up the shackles and obeyed.

"Now stand next to Ellen. Run the cuffs through the metal bar and put the open end around Ellen's right wrist," Jake said. "Toss that pistol into the outboard."

Welch's weapon bounced off the hull's insulating lagging and clinked against pipes on its way to the bilge.

Jake picked up a microphone and signaled Kao.

"Rover, come to CAMP," he said.

★

Kao whispered orders.

"Mister Jaguar, lower level," he said. "Mister Leopard and Mister Panther, third level. I will handle second level. Move!"

As Kao swept through the compartment's second level, he glanced between the tubes and caught a glimpse of Jake's handcuffed prisoners on the other side. He high-stepped over bunking racks that protruded into the passageway.

Checking for stray crewmen, he brushed each rack's privacy curtain aside with the silencer of his M-16 rifle. Finding no one, he reached the forward bulkhead of the missile compartment.

Jaguar, like the other commandos, had just graduated with the latest class of Taiwan's Para-Frogmen special forces.

A deck below Kao, on the third level, Jaguar watched his compatriots, Leopard and Panther, trot down a corridor between the missile tubes that separated the crew's bunkrooms.

Alone, Jaguar scanned the empty machinery space before hopping down a steel ladder into the submarine's depths.

His bare foot touched the cold steel deck plates of the compartment's lower level. He stared down a central walkway lined by gas-generators, man-sized cylinders of explosives used to jettison and launch Trident Missiles.

Seeing no activity, Jaguar trotted along the centerline corridor. He passed each missile tube and gas generator in hypnotic repetition, listening to the rhythmic cadence of his footsteps echoing through the bilge under his feet.

The commando passed between missiles one and two and stopped at the watertight bulkhead of the forward compartment. Pipes, hoses, and valves wove a tangled mural around him. Jaguar found the endless mechanical jungle of the *Colorado* alien.

Squatting below a ladder, he leaned his rifle against his thigh and waited until he saw Leopard's masked face above. Leopard offered a thumbs up, indicating that he and Panther had found no one in the crew's bunkrooms.

The eleven-man team of Kao's men, Jake's *Colorado* accomplices, and Renard controlled the engine room and the missile compartment. Only the forward compartment and a few dozen tired men separated them from control of the submarine.

Ducking through a machined circular door into the forward compartment, Jake turned into the missile control center. Towers of aging computers spanned the dimensions of a racquetball court. Two sailors sat at panels that directed the launching and guidance systems.

"What's up Mister Slate? We heard the rover paged twice," Missile Technician First Class Brady asked.

"I found him. You guys alone?" Jake asked.

"Yes, sir. Everyone who's not on watch should still be in the crew's mess."

"Good. Now get up," Jake said and pulled the pistol from behind his back. "I'm stealing the ship - with some help."

Jake sensed the all-black image of Kao in his wetsuit, ski mask, and sunglasses slide beside him and raise a silenced M-16 rifle.

Jake tossed a pair of handcuffs to Brady.

"Cuff yourselves together."

"You've got to be kidding," Brady said.

Jake aligned his pistol's rear and barrel sites with Brady's thigh and squeezed the trigger. A kick recoiled at his wrist, a silencer whined, and crimson splashed from dark blue trousers.

"You bastard!" Brady said.

"He's serious. Just do what he says," the other sailor said while tightening the cuffs around his wrist.

"Good," Jake said. "Now step outside with my colleague, head to CAMP, and cuff your free hands like Ellen and Welch."

Jake moved deeper into the forward compartment and yelled for the final watchman.

"Belowdecks! This is the duty officer. Belowdecks watchman, can you hear me?"

Jake dug the silencer of his pistol into his belt at the small of his back and tiptoed up a staircase to the control room. The belowdecks watchman, a pudgy, acne-faced teenager, sat at a panel copying data into his logbook.

"Sir?" Seaman Williams asked.

"I know you're busy, but I need you to come to the crew's mess," Jake said.

"The security drill was that bad, huh?"

"Yeah."

"Sir, do you smell gunpowder?"

The residue in my pistol, Jake thought.

Jake raised his fingers to his nose and sniffed.

"Yeah. I think I smell it, too. It's probably because the duty chief and I ran an inventory of the gun locker after the drill. That locker stinks."

"I'll say. What do you need, sir?"

"Finish taking your logs later. Just hurry on down and join the rest of the guys."

Jake backed down the ladder. At the bottom, he pressed against a wall to keep his weapon hidden.

"Williams, tell the crew I'll be there soon."

Jake retraced his steps to Kao and led him down a stairway to the crew's mess. He overheard his duty chief keeping the duty section under control.

"Look, I know he's been gone a while, but the belowdecks watchman just said Mister Slate was coming back. Quit whining. I know you're all tired, but we'll be able to hit the rack soon."

Jake entered the mess and stood behind a table that would serve as a barrier against any would-be heroes.

"Where have you been, sir? We missed you," the duty chief said.

Jake surveyed the duty crew, a fraction of the entire ship's complement. The fatigue in their faces confirmed their desire to return to their racks to sleep.

"I know you're mad that I ran the drill," Jake said.

He waved his pistol over his head. Fifty-six bleary eyes opened wide.

"I'm stealing the *Colorado*. If you want to live, keep your mouths shut and do what I tell you."

Jake nodded as Kao slid through a back doorway.

"This is some sick joke, right?" the duty chief asked.

Jake leveled the pistol at the man's leg and squeezed off a round.

Flesh wounds heal, he thought. *Pain and fear will keep them disciplined. Discipline will keep them alive.*

"I said, keep your damn mouths shut! You will all remain here under guard while I get the ship underway. If you speak or move without being told, my men will kill you."

The fear in the crew's eyes told Jake that they believed him.

"When instructed, you will enter the missile compartment, take the ladder to second level, and then go to the missile compartment hatch," Jake said. "Once there, you will don life jackets and head topside. En route, you will free the men handcuffed at CAMP."

Jake tossed the handcuff keys onto the nearest table.

"When you are topside, you will jump overboard and swim to land. The strong swimmers will help the weak and the injured. You may jump overboard whenever you want, but I'll secure the screw so you don't get sucked under. A man at every corner of your evacuation route will prevent any stupid ideas of heroism. If you have to use the head, go in your pants."

Jaguar stepped beside Jake. Leopard and Panther slid behind Kao.

"Remember, keep your damn mouths shut! No talking. Nod your heads if you understand."

As heads nodded, Jake looked at Kao.

"Let's get this pig to sea."

CHAPTER TWO

JANUARY 6, 2006
DETERRENT PATROL AREA, ATLANTIC OCEAN:

THE USS COLORADO'S EIGHTEEN THOUSAND tons carved a conical swath through the Atlantic Ocean. Seven stories tall at its conning tower sail, the submarine shouldered twenty-four Trident D-5 ballistic missiles, an arsenal of nuclear destruction born of Cold War nightmares.

Few people knew more about the *Colorado* than the twenty-six year old naval officer from Connecticut, Lieutenant Jacob Slate, who preferred that his friends call him 'Jake'.

Four months prior to his seizing of the vessel, Jake had considered the *Colorado* a second home and its crew like a family. He had been a model officer, but that was about to change.

★

As Jake descended a stairwell en route to the *Colorado's* wardroom, a lanky, dark-haired man caught his eye. He stared at a grimy face.

"McKenzie, you been playing in the lube oil tanks again?" Jake asked.

"No, sir. Diesel fuel oil tank. Can we talk? In the machinery room?"

Jake followed McKenzie down a ladder.

Electric generators whirred. A refrigeration compressor caged within silvery piping droned. Jake welcomed the familiar sounds that kept conversations private and rested his hand on Scott McKenzie's shoulder.

"You stupid shit," Jake said. "Who else knows you're banging a shipmate's wife?"

"I'm not banging her. I love her. You don't understand," McKenzie said.

"You've got a good heart, Scotty, but you're also a twenty-two year old swinging dick."

A sound like snapping bamboo cracked. A hiss followed. Jake cringed and gazed at a junior mechanic crawling around piping in the back of the room.

"What the hell's Hicks doing?" he asked.

"Dumping the accumulator on the external hydraulic plant," McKenzie said.

"I thought we fixed it twice already this patrol."

"It's broke again."

"We'll check on Hicks in a minute. We still have your problem to deal with."

"What should I do?" McKenzie asked.

"The last time a guy had an affair with a crewman's wife they found him left for dead in the bilge. If you stay here, this is going to leak out. We're going to have to transfer you before the next patrol."

"I don't want to leave."

"It's too late," Jake said. "Everyone on this old steel pig likes you, and I'm going to miss you, but I don't want to scrape your corpse out of the bilge."

"I can't leave. She needs me. He doesn't love her anymore. He's cheating on her and-"

"And banging her is going to make it better?"

Thunder rang from the back of the room. Hicks, the junior mechanic, stumbled through a spray of oil. Jake trotted toward him, stopped at an emergency circuit, and tore the handset from its cradle.

"Hydraulic rupture, machinery room!" Jake said.

"Hydraulic rupture in the machinery room," the ship-wide speaker said over the hydraulic hiss. *"Ascending to periscope depth to ventilate."*

The hissing died.

"I got it!" McKenzie said. "Relief valve shut. Leak isolated."

"Sir, I was dumping the accumulator when the relief lifted," Hicks said.

Over the ringing in his ears Jake discerned the chopping of pumps that pounded the hydraulic plant.

"You left the pumps on!" Jake said and reached for a red 'off' button.

He saw aging, bent piping bulge just before it ruptured and launched copper shards. His forehead smacked an electrical panel and his shoulder slammed metal.

Lacerations burned deep within him. His knees splashed into a chocolate colored pool of oil and blood. He fell into McKenzie's arms and slipped into unconsciousness.

Jake awoke under the lights of the *Colorado*'s wardroom. He felt a tug at his blood-soaked sleeve and heard scissors ripping cotton. Dizzy, he recognized the *Colorado*'s corpsman.

"It's not pretty. I'm going to try to patch you up," the corpsman said.

Out of the corner of his eye, Jake saw the large figure of Commander Thomas Henry enter the room. He wondered if his commanding officer cared or was feigning requisite concern. As morphine saturated him, he accepted Henry's image as the Angel of Death.

Jake awoke again on the wardroom table. Pillows canted him toward his uninjured left side, and an intravenous tube fed him fluid.

"Don't move, Mister Slate," a medical technician said. "There's still metal in you."

"I can feel it," Jake said.

"I'm calling the corpsman. Don't move, sir."

"Holy shit, Jake," a man said. "You look like crap."

"Thanks, Riley. You don't look much better," Jake said while craning his neck to see his friend, Lieutenant Riley Demorse.

Demorse's chestnut hair was disheveled. Green eyes beamed through dark circles painted over olive skin.

"I had the midnight watch. Dude, you're so lucky Walker is our corpsman. He says you're still low on blood, but you should be okay until we can evacuate you."

Jake trembled at the thought of his mortality, and metal shards heightened his sensations as the *Colorado* vibrated at its top speed.

"Feels like we're running at a flank bell."

"Yeah, to get you out of here. We're dumping you off in Bermuda, you son of a bitch. You get a free ride off this pig via helicopter. We've already relinquished nuclear target coverage to the *Maryland* so we can dump your ass off. I'm so jealous except-"

"Except what?"

"Well," Demorse said. "I've got bad news – or maybe it's good news – depending on your sense of humor."

Demorse recounted the story of how the ship's corpsman and volunteers from the crew rallied to save him. Jake's sense of humor was dark, and it had helped him stomach plenty of bad news in his life. But during the moments of silence that followed his friend's tale, he wished he had died on the wardroom table.

★

A month passed, and Jake's flesh had recovered from his injuries on the *Colorado*, but he was only beginning to understand how the accident would continue to destroy him.

He tried to clear the accident from his mind by riding his dirt bike in a power line clearing outside the naval submarine base in Kings Bay, Georgia. The *Colorado* had returned, and his friend Riley Demorse joined him.

Jake shielded his eyes from the sunlight reflecting off Demorse's helmet. Foam helmet pads flipped tufts of chestnut hair as Riley took off the helmet. Steam rose from Demorse's Honda four-stroke XR-250 dirt bike.

"You've got to be kidding me. You're not going to do it?" Demorse asked.

Jake pointed his motorcycle at a ramp that rose above the sage grass. He revved his Kawasaki KX-500 two stroke monster - a beast that few riders dared push to its mechanical limits.

"You're nuts!" Riley said.

Jake bent forward and gunned the green monster's single piston engine. The motor howled a chainsaw chorus. Blue-gray smoke from the black muffler wafted over him. Leather-gloved hands gripped rubber handles.

Jake kicked the gear shifter down straight into second gear. He relaxed his fingers and popped the clutch shut. The drive train clicked. The chain snapped taut. A knobby tire spewed earth.

Jake's head snapped, and moist air whipped over his mouth guard and abraded his cheeks. He pulled the twist-throttle back and ripped the bike through second gear. He tapped the clutch and kicked the Kawasaki into third.

Engine howling, the Kawasaki hit the ramp. The handlebar jerked upward, jammed Jake's arms, and stunned him.

He awoke in ballistic flight and felt his stomach ten feet below. He looked down and tried to align the bike, but the front wheel swung high. He tapped the brake pedal, and the wheel lowered but slanted as it hit the ground. The landing tore the bike from under him and catapulted him over the handlebars.

His shoulder hit the ground and his helmet slapped hard earth. Sprawling on the dirt, Jake felt numb. As he began to feel his body, he performed a self-assessment. All limbs were attached and working, but he throbbed everywhere and his wrist burned. Nothing felt broken, and he judged the rush worth the pain.

"That was awesome," Demorse said. "You're a lunatic!"

"Hey, if you're not biking above your abilities, you're not biking," Jake said.

"Let me help you up, dude," Riley said.

"Just get the fuck away!"

Jake felt horrible the second he snapped. The accident at the *Colorado's* hydraulic plant had turned every waking moment into a battle to control his anger.

"Easy, killer," Demorse said. "What's wrong?"

"Look, Riley, I didn't mean to take it out on you, but I've got some serious shit on my mind."

"Like what?"

Jake stood and limped to his bike. Oozing oil glistened on the engine. He grabbed the handlebars and walked the Kawasaki back to Demorse.

"Like I'm trying to figure out how to beat our commanding officer to death and get away with it."

"Shit, Jake," Demorse said. "I hate him, too, but I wouldn't kill him. What's going on?"

"There's more wrong than you know," Jake said. "And it wasn't all an accident."

CHAPTER THREE

TEN YEARS AGO, PIERRE RENARD had retired as one of France's most decorated submarine commanders. The French Navy's top brass had pegged him for flag rank, but Renard found the political and administrative constraints of the admiralty too confining. He had greater plans.

Using his retired officer network, he had become a director for the French shipbuilder DCN International in its *Agosta* submarine program delivery to Pakistan. While succeeding with the *Agosta* delivery, Renard had established relations with senior Pakistani military officials. After impressing them with recommendations on military planning, he had met with then-General Pervez Musharraf himself.

Renard's French nationality had brought a detached objectiveness that the Pakistani leader valued. By the time Renard had explained a fraction of his analysis of the Pakistani defense structure, Musharraf had offered to quadruple his salary to leave DCN and join his staff. Renard had accepted the job on the spot.

Renard had addressed gaps in Pakistan's ability to integrate their military operations. He had convinced Musharraf to coordinate his air defenses with his ground and naval forces and had urged him to accelerate the Super-7 aircraft's production before the United States could pressure China to terminate delivery. As conflict in the Kashmir region validated Renard's counsel, a grateful Musharraf had showered the Frenchman with bonuses. Then he had sent him to Algeria.

In Algiers, Renard had used his brokering skills to prevent Russia from adding delays and surcharges to their agreement to deliver their *Kilo* class submarines - as they had done with Iran. After helping Algeria acquire its foremost naval weapons, Renard had assisted with training its crews, developing its tactics, and transferring knowledge about the *Kilos* to Musharraf's admirals to use against the *Kilos* of the Indian fleet.

Success in Algeria garnered an invitation from an Iranian admiral to upgrade his *Kilo* fleet tactics, and then an Iranian general asked him to outline and acquire the means to improve his anti-air defenses. By the time he had left Iran for his subsequent client, Renard had become a renowned international military consultant and arms dealer.

As the money flowed into his personal coffers and his ego grew with the demand for his services, Renard had developed a power base, network, and reputation among many countries dotting the map between his first two Pakistani and Algerian clients. But after a decade of strengthening the militaries of former-soviet states and countries across Africa, Renard had felt himself trapped.

Although raised in a Christian democracy, Renard had found no moral problem in assisting undemocratic Islamic states, but when rebel factions and thugs started seeking him, requests had become orders, and threats had followed his attempts at refusal.

Two years ago, he had awoken in Nigeria with the dark epiphany that he had created a mobilized and integrated anti-air defense network for a gang of brutes. When his captors had released him, Renard had returned to France and made the crucial decision to leave the money and power behind, dismantle his network, and retire.

But as he had reflected upon his career, the impact his work had imparted upon the world had depressed him. To make restitution, he had decided to undertake a final planning and weapons acquisition operation that would begin to redeem the acts he regretted. Decades as a Cold War warrior had made him an anti-communist, and he decided that he would transform Taiwan, communist China's adversary, into a nuclear state.

★

MARCH 26, 2006
FIFTEEN NAUTICAL MILES NORTH OF PETRAPOVLOSK, RUSSIA

Renard knelt in a bobbing Zodiac and cringed as the Bering Sea's breeze invaded his parka.

"*Merde!*" he said. "My testicles have frozen into cannon shot."

The sea nudged his Zodiac against the fishing trawler he had purchased weeks ago. Renard glanced over his shoulder. Rubber boots dangled over the ship's edge.

"Yes?" the man in the boots asked.

"I was merely making conversation with myself since you and your companions are boring."

The man and his boots walked away.

Renard kept his eyes on the trawler. He had tested it on gale force seas and conducted crashback runs on its diesel engines, shifting from a flank bell to full reverse to verify the boat's integrity. He trusted the trawler more than the Taiwanese sailors with whom he shared it.

I've earned reward for taking risks, he thought as he shifted his weight to flush blood through his legs. *But I can hardly wait to finish this and retire.*

A chime rang near his chest. He slipped his fingers from his glove, reached for his wireless phone, and pressed it against his cheek.

"Hello?"

"Are you there...with the trawler and Zodiacs?" Major Alexander Chernokov asked.

"Yes. All is prepared."

"Then it begins," Chernokov said.

"I wish you luck, my friend," Renard said. "God willing, I will see you soon."

★

Red cheeks and fair skin gave Russian Major Alexander Chernokov an appearance younger than his thirty-nine years. Given his freedom, he would have pursued a doctorate in his passion of astrophysics, but paternal pressure from a decorated infantry officer had forced him into the military. While his contemporaries with genuine military interest became colonels, Chernokov became sour.

He ran Petropavlovsk's security detachment in the Russian Far East, distant from the comforts of Moscow. His salary, when paid, bought only secondhand goods for his family of four. Electricity and water were often rationed.

After years of discontent and no sign of promotion, Chernokov felt little guilt in selling ten SSN-18 nuclear warheads to Renard for three million dollars and a new life outside Russia.

★

A three-vehicle convoy climbed a dirt incline. Its lead jeep's headlights illuminated a hillside. As Chernokov's driver circumvented a rut, the beams lit the tops of oak trees and the road's dirt shoulder crept up to the vehicle's tires.

Pulse racing, Chernokov withdrew a Taser from his pocket and slammed it against his driver's chest. The driver convulsed and fell limp against his door.

As the jeep rolled to a stop, Chernokov reached into the glove compartment for a plastic box that contained syringes loaded with the analgesic drug fentanyl, made infamous when Chechen rebels overtook a Moscow theater. He popped one syringe into his driver's thigh, opened his door, and jumped to the ground.

He looked through the windshield of the transport truck behind him. Its driver convulsed as Chernokov's accomplice, Captain Victor Ivanovich, shocked his victim. Ivanovich tugged the driver to the floor and grasped the wheel. Chernokov joined Ivanovich in the ten-wheeler and placed his boots on the unconscious driver.

"Reverse. Now!" Chernokov said.

The engine growled, and the truck lurched and slammed into the trailing jeep. Chernokov stuck his head out the window and watched the jeep tumble into the ravine.

Ivanovich stopped the ten-wheeler and jumped out. Chernokov reached into his jacket for a flashbang grenade. He yanked the pin and held a spring-released detonator. A bulletproof panel opened behind him, and light flowed through the gap.

"What's going on?" asked a soldier from the infantry squadron sealed in the warhead compartment.

Chernokov tossed the flashbang grenade through the hole. Thunder cracked. With the guards incapacitated, he reached into his jacket for a vial of fentanyl in its gaseous form, opened it, and tossed it into the cargo cabin.

Chernokov stuck his head outside the ten-wheeler and watched a flashbang grenade leave Ivanovich's hand and land in the ravine. An explosion rocked the toppled jeep. Ivanovich stood like a zombie as one of the four men from the trailing jeep staggered to all fours. The remaining men lay on the ground.

"Round them up," Chernokov said. "I expect little resistance in doping these incapacitated men with the fentanyl vials, but if any man should regain consciousness and defy you, shoot him in the belly."

"We will leave them here?" Ivanovich asked.

"Yes. They will not awake in time to stop us."

"This drug can be fatal," Ivanovich said.

"I've measured the dosage, and these men are strong," Chernokov said. "Most, if not all, will survive."

★

Renard listened to Chernokov's voice on his wireless.

"It is done," Chernokov said. "We are approaching."

"Well done! I will soon reunite you with your family as a very wealthy man," Renard said.

The Frenchman scanned the rocky shore in anticipation of Chernokov's arrival. He trembled as anxiety heightened the chill.

"What's delaying the other Zodiac?" he asked the man in the rubber boots above.

Hearing no response irked Renard. He had expected more enthusiasm from the men the Taiwanese Deputy Defense Minister had lent him to steal warheads for their country.

He raised his gaze to a sailor's scowl.

"Well, what's the delay?" he asked.

"The other Zodiac is in the water," the sailor said. "Your Russian man - he has begun his attack?"

"Yes," Renard said as he untied the Zodiac from the trawler. "They have the warheads. Let's make for shore!"

As Renard reached for the Zodiac's motor controls, a bullet whistled by his ear. Fire burned in his back and he fell to the Zodiac's deck. Two bursts of gunfire echoed off the tree line.

As the fire in his flesh became numbness, he heard yelling in Mandarin. He bit the glove off the hand he could feel, reached into his parka, and withdrew his pistol. He aimed at the conversation above him and pulled the trigger.

Bullets clanked against the trawler. The engines droned and propellers swished. By the time Renard unloaded his clip he was alone. He collapsed and stared at the stars through the mist of his shallow breaths.

He propped himself on his good arm and examined his chest. Blood trickled from an exit wound. He knew he would survive the injury but doubted he would survive the Russian military if discovered.

Feeling returned to his arm, and he groped through his parka for a Marlboro. Popping one into his mouth, he worked a gold-plated Zippo lighter. Flicking the lid, he whipped his thumb across a gear that sparked flint into flame. Nicotine stifled the butterflies in his stomach. He reached for his wireless phone.

★

As Chernokov drove the truck full of warheads along a grass-covered forest road, he heard the rear doors clanking as they vented fentanyl.

He placed his wireless to his ear.

"Yes?"

"We've been betrayed," Renard said. "I've been shot and abandoned. We must abort."

Chernokov's stomach knotted.

"I will retrieve you both," Renard said. "I have two Zodiacs, and I've memorized the local charts. We can make for Petrapovlosk or perhaps the fishing havens to commandeer a trawler."

Chernokov gaped at the moonlit silhouette of a KA-52 Hokum attack helicopter. Rotor wash whipped treetops, and turboshaft engines whined. A troop transport helicopter rose behind the Hokum and descended behind the trees.

The Hokum hovered in front of Chernokov.

"Jump!" he said.

The Hokum's twin 30-millimeter guns erupted. The rounds splintered branches, shattered the ten-wheeler's windshield, and shredded Ivanovich.

Chernokov leapt, rolled, and scampered into underbrush. Through the trees, he saw soldiers approaching. He cursed and lifted the wireless to his ear.

"Are you still with me?" he asked.

"Yes, of course," Renard said. "What's happening? I hear chopper blades and cannon fire."

"There are ground troops...a Hokum...Victor is dead."

"*Merde*! I'm sorry for Victor, but we must make haste. Meet at our rendezvous point. Circle through the trees to the south and-"

"You would risk your life for me?"

"I've never betrayed an ally. The Zodiac will be hard to see, and it is fast. We can escape."

Chernokov heard an infantry officer barking commands to the squad of soldiers.

"Save yourself," he said. "Find a fisherman's house two miles to the north. Pitevski...he will hide you. At daybreak, find a merchant, Yvgeni Kuznetsov. As a contingency, I paid Kuznetsov in advance."

"No, you must join me," Renard said. "Make for shore."

"You will inform my family of my love for them."

"No, do what you must. Run! Swim to me! I got you into this. I will get you out."

"You will ensure my family's well-being?"

"Circle to the south. I will meet you."

"Promise me...my family's future," Chernokov said.

He knelt by a pine and unscrewed the silencer from his pistol. A deep sigh issued from the phone.

"I promise you my friend," Renard said. "They will want for nothing."

The words comforted Chernokov as he chose his fate.

Renard pressed a palm against his exit wound and drove the Zodiac northward. A crack of gunfire shot from the trees, startled him, and died in the sea's blackness.

Although the Russian traitor had been an instrument in his chess game, two years of befriending and promising Chernokov a better life weighed on Renard's conscience.

"My God," he said. "What have I done?"

CHAPTER FOUR

THE SHUTTLE BOUNCED THROUGH TURBULENCE and jostled the wound in Pierre Renard's shoulder. A salmon fisher's wife had bandaged his wound so that he could delay professional attention until he could find a private physician.

He studied the passenger beside him. Thick eyebrows cast shadows across the eyes of Yvgeni Kuznetsov, a wealthy Russian exporter. A scar cut through pockmarks on Kuznetsov's cheek.

"Fortunately," Renard said, "the pain in my wound keeps me awake. Lord knows that you're not providing lively companionship."

"I attended to your safety after you led my friend to his death," Kuznetsov said.

"Chernokov accepted the risks."

"You seduced a desperate but good man to his death."

Fumbling for his Marlboros, Renard realized that he was wearing Kuznetsov's clothes. The beige dress shirt and tweed blazer held no cigarettes to calm him, but he was relieved to feel his lighter, his wallet, and his encrypted cell phone.

"Then why are you helping me?" he asked.

"Chernokov asked me to prepare an evacuation in case your plan failed. He made me swear to take you or Ivanovich to the States in case he did not survive. I am carrying out the last wishes of the friend you killed."

"I assume he paid you well?" Renard asked.

Kuznetsov folded his copy of <u>Fortune</u>.

"I will use my connections to assist you through Customs," the Russian said. "After that, my obligation ends. If I see you in Russia again, I will see that you are strangled by your own intestines."

★

Outside Anchorage International Airport, Renard called his Parisian office in the 5th Arondissement, southwest of the Pont Neuf. As his cell phone rang, he envisioned Marie Broyer, his assistant and lover.

Marie's image teased his mind. Her brown hair fell in waves to rounded breasts. The pastel dresses she preferred highlighted her narrow waist and shapely hips. High cheekbones and petulant lips complemented a striking face.

Her beauty, refinement, and reliability made the thirty-five year old Sorbonne-educated doctor of languages irresistible to Renard.

"Hello, Verincourt Enterprises," she said in French.

Her throaty voice revealed that he had awoken her.

"It's me," he said. "We're encrypted. Speak freely."

"It's good to hear your voice," Marie said. "I was worried."

A cab stopped curbside, and a uniformed attendant opened the door. Renard shook his head, shifted his phone to his other ear, and walked away.

"I hear automobile tires," Marie said. "You're not where I expected you to be."

"The operation was a failure," he said. "I'm lucky to have escaped with my life. The others are dead."

While he let Marie absorb the news, Renard used his free hand to maneuver a Marlboro to his lips. He sparked flame from his Zippo lighter and inhaled the tobacco taste.

"Dead? How?"

"The Russian Army. A Chinese mole must have infiltrated the Taiwanese Defense Ministry and informed the Russians. I suspect one of the Minister's deputies, but I will find out for myself when I return to Taipei."

"You were nearly killed, and now you want to return to Taipei? Foolhardy. The Taiwanese are perfectly capable of taking care of themselves. Come home."

Renard was exhausted and in pain. He lowered the phone and vented his frustration to the Alaskan cold.

"Damn it, woman. How many times have we been through this? I must arm Taiwan to reset the balance. I was blinded by greed and pride and spent the last ten years arming the wrong side. I must set this straight."

He returned the phone to his ear.

"You were mumbling," she said.

"I was just...lamenting. All this time invested into an operation, and to have it fail like this."

"You must feel terrible," she said.

"Those men I lost yesterday - they were my recruits, but they had become like friends. Ivanovich had no family, but I must see to..."

A sour taste filled his mouth. Blaming the cigarette, he tossed it to the pavement and fumbled through his blazer for a new one.

"...the Chernokov widow and orphans."

"How are you taking this all?" she asked.

Renard inhaled and watched smoke from his fresh cigarette twist in the gray sky.

"How do you expect me to take it? When I commanded a submarine, I had my tactical steps mapped out better than my adversary. In every arms deal I've brokered, I've known my client's military needs better than he. But betrayal? Dead colleagues? I've never been caught so off my guard. I must start over with nothing."

"Start over?" she asked. "You expect to stumble across another opportunity to acquire nuclear weapons?"

"I have moles in intelligence agencies, contacts in the weapons community, and a strong client relationship with the Taiwanese Minister of Defense. It will take time, but I will arm Taiwan."

"I admire your determination and optimism," she said.

Renard ignored Marie's assessment and shifted his thoughts to moving forward.

"One of our wireless phones is lying on Chernokov's corpse. We need to erase Verincourt Enterprises and all aliases and records associated with it. I trust you know what to do."

"Of course," she said. "I will shift our operations to the business in Lyon."

"Good. Once in Lyon, contact all my resources – moles, business colleagues, past clients, even old naval shipmates. Perhaps an opportunity has arisen while I was focused on my Russian warhead operation."

"Warhead theft, you mean."

"If you disapprove of my ways, then why do you stay with me?"

"Because I...you pay me well."

Renard mustered as much compassion as he could spare.

"I know what you want from me," he said. "But you know that I refuse to settle down until I close this deal with Taiwan, and my resolve is only stronger after coming so close."

"Perhaps I can accelerate things," she said.

"How?"

"You underestimate me," Marie said. "While you were in the field, I maintained contact with several of your moles. I believe I may have found an opportunity."

"You kept looking? I'm not sure if I should commend your diligence or reprimand your lack of faith in me."

"Do neither," she said. "I know that you will never be mine until you satisfy yourself that you've restructured the balance of power in the Pacific Ocean to your liking. Consider it a self-serving act of insurance."

Excited, Renard stamped out his half-smoked Marlboro and lit a fresh one.

"Well?" he asked. "What opportunity?"

"Your CIA analyst mole has been busy. You must have impressed her on your last recruiting trip to the States. I imagine that she's beautiful, is she not?"

"No, she's hideous and weighs one hundred kilos if she weighs a gram," he said. "That's why it's so easy. The money helps, too."

"You're a scoundrel."

"What did she find?"

"One of her databanks indicated that an American naval officer was removed from the nuclear weapons stewardship program for emotional instability. There was a tip from an anonymous source that he had threatened the life of his commanding officer, but he was returned to full duty with a generic explanation. Removal is rare, and return to duty without a detailed list of reasons is abnormal."

Renard's mind cranked into motion.

"This hints of a buried truth – possibly an ugly one," he said. "Do you know what weapons he oversees?"

"He's stationed on a Trident Missile submarine."

"Excellent," he said. "The U.S. Navy pushes nuclear responsibility much farther down the chain of command than their other branches. I want you to make contact with the officer."

"Me? What would you have me do?"

"Investigate his condition," Renard said. "If he's emotionally unstable, there's a reason for it. I want you to find out what it is."

"Why should I do it?" Marie asked.

"He's young, is he not?"

"Wait."

Renard heard Marie flipping through her notes and thought of her handwriting. When she was happy her handwriting flowed with long strokes and wide curves, but when she felt used, her writing became robotic.

"He's twenty-six," she said.

"Still a walking hormone," Renard said. "Unlike Chernokov, he's taking in a respectable salary. I'm sure that I will ultimately need money to recruit him, but if he's emotionally frustrated, initial contact needs to target his weakness. For a man his age that means sex."

"You would have me mount him and grind at his loins until he screams out his darkest secrets?"

"The illusion of sex will suffice," he said. "You have your sex appeal, your charm, and your wit. Approach him, convince him you care about him, and extract a little honesty from the man. He will find you attractive, and being nearly a decade older, you will represent maternal concern to his subconscious. He will confide in you."

"And if the illusion of sex fails?"

Renard chuckled.

"Modern submarine fleets are staffed by men of strong mind and will, not necessarily of strong body. Chances are that I would end up pitying you if the illusion fails, but I expect you to extract the information any way you can."

"Do you really think you can use him to get your hands on American nuclear weapons?" she asked.

"You doubted I could use Chernokov to get to Russian weapons," he said, "and I almost had them in my damned hands. I know how to create possibilities."

"Okay," Marie said. "I will serve as your whore, but if he happens to be gorgeous, you will have no right to an iota of jealousy if I must sleep with him."

The line went dead.

★

The next morning, Renard took a plane from Anchorage to San Francisco International. Then he took a taxi to a four star hotel where he had reserved a room for weeks. An apprehensive woman opened the suite's door.

Renard said nothing. His arrival three weeks early without a Russian officer beside him conveyed the news that Chernokov's widow feared. She grabbed his arms and dug her fingers into his skin. Her thumbnail grated his bullet wound, and he accepted the pain as his penance.

"He loved you. He died bravely. I'm sorry," he said in crude Russian.

The woman collapsed and wailed.

Renard reached into his breast pocket and lowered a piece of paper with a name and number on it.

"This man will advise you about your money."

She spat her anger too quickly for Renard to comprehend, but he read the hatred in her eyes.

"I'm sorry," he said as he retreated. When he was alone, he vowed — not for the first time — to create no more widows.

CHAPTER FIVE

As Jake returned his mud-covered off-road motorcycle to the garage, his cell phone rang. He ducked into his Jeep Grand Cherokee, rifled through his duffle bag, and answered the phone.

He heard a friendly voice.

"Hey, Jake. It's John Brody. How are you?"

"Good to hear from the master and commander of the *Miami*," he said.

"Best submarine in the world."

"Why is it you sound like you have a shit-eating grin on your face?" Jake asked.

"Because I do," Brody said.

Talking to Brody usually made Jake feel confident and upbeat, but not today.

"Not in the mood for games," Jake said.

"Okay. I've got a main seawater valve that won't shut all the way, and I'm bringing the *Miami* in for dry dock repairs at Kings Bay. I'm in that cockamamie swizzle stick of a waterway you guys call a navigable channel."

"Right now?"

Jake heard the wind whipping over Brody's receiver and knew he had asked a stupid question.

"Yes, right now. I'm on the bridge with my fingers crossed that I don't beach my boat in the sand. I don't know how the heck you guys steam through this channel in those bloated Trident submarines."

"You'll be fine," Jake said.

"Yeah," Brody said. "I know. I should tie to the pier in about an hour."

"How long are you going to be here?"

"The dry docks are full up in New London, so I'm going to get all my preventative maintenance done while I'm here. Several weeks at least."

"Carole's not going to like that," Jake said.

Brody's voice became a baritone whisper.

"I wanted to tell you over a beer," Brody said. "Carole is leaving me. No one else knows yet."

Jake remembered the last Christmas he had spent with the Brodys. He flipped his wallet open to a picture of John and Carole Brody wearing the matching sweaters he had given them. Nothing seemed to be going right.

"Let's hang out tonight," Brody said "I need to drown my sorrows."

"Sure. You want to go out in St. Marys or head down to Jacksonville?"

"Local," Brody said. "Let's keep it simple."

★

Jake and Brody passed through the dining room and onto the hardwood floor where patrons could order pitchers of beer and eat casual food in Seagle's Waterfront Café, a pub outside the Kings Bay Naval Submarine Base. It was a weekday and the clientele was sparse.

Brody kicked back his second draft beer while Jake was still sipping his first.

"Come on," Brody said. "You've got to keep up with me."

"I have no problem with pickling myself if that's what you want to do," Jake said. "If anyone's got a right to drink, it's you."

"I didn't know who else to talk to," Brody said.

"So what set Carole off?" Jake asked.

"She says I'm a failure and that I drink too much."

"What made her say that?"

"I keep a bottle of whiskey in my stateroom, and the crew knows about it. So does my commodore."

"That's serious, but isn't it an unwritten law that commanding officers are allowed to indulge now and then?"

"Maybe in the old days. Not anymore."

"What's this failure crap about?" Jake asked.

"The selection board convened. I didn't make captain. I only have one shot left, and it's a long shot."

"The selection board is a bunch of morons."

"Let's drop it. Tell me what's up with you."

Jake tipped back his beer.

"You probably read an accident report about a hydraulic plant rupture," he said.

"That wasn't you, was it?"

Jake stood, lifted his shirt, and exposed a series of scars on his back.

"Damn!" Brody said. "How are you?"

"Life's good, despite my little injury," Jake said. "Full recovery. I'm running and lifting again and even riding the dirt bike. I have one more patrol before rotating to admiral's aide duty for Sublant."

"You're going to be the aide for the commander of the Atlantic Submarine Fleet? That's a great career move."

Would have been, Jake thought. *Won't happen now.*

"I talked to your executive officer a few months ago," Brody said. "He said you're the best tactician he's seen."

"You called my executive officer?"

"He was my plebe at the Academy. I was just checking up on him. I thought I'd check on you while I had the chance."

A waitress came by, and Jake ordered another pitcher and two shots of tequila. Jake's mind wandered through a haze of inebriation. He studied the lounge and fixed his gaze on an attractive redhead in her mid-thirties clad in a tight sweater and jeans. He stared until her pale blue eyes caught his.

Ashamed, he turned away, although he saw her smile and flip her hair over her shoulder.

Three men dressed in Dockers and sweaters approached. Each greeted Brody as 'Captain', the traditional term for a commanding officer, and a crowd formed around the table.

"Hey guys," Brody said. "What are you doing here?"

"Just a bunch of sailors in port prowling around town, Captain. There aren't a whole lot of places to drink around here, so we figured we'd find you," a tall lieutenant named Brian Keller said.

"You mind if we throw some down with you, sir?" asked Lieutenant Carlos Fernandez.

Brody made introductions and Lieutenant Keller's eyes got big.

"You're the one who saved the skipper?" he asked.

"Well, I helped," Jake said.

"Bullshit," Brody said.

The swearing told Jake that Brody was drunk.

"You saved my ass and don't be shy about taking credit."

The group huddled to listen.

"What is it now?" Brody asked. "Almost four years ago?"

"Yeah," Jake said. "Almost."

"I had just finished my executive officer tour on the *Florida* and took over as a battalion officer at the Naval Academy," Brody said. "Having earned my commission at a superior academic institution-"

"Notre Dame? That's hilarious, Captain," Fernandez said.

"Pipe down, 'Purdue'," Brody said. "Anyway, I didn't know the culture at the academy, so I just enforced the policies the commandant told me to enforce. Apparently, I built up the reputation as a hard-ass."

"That's an understatement," Jake said.

"Anyway, no one can argue that I did the right thing by having a midshipman expelled for slapping a black plebe. Since I was the ranking black man on staff, word about the incident got to me first, and I took care of it."

"A lot of people respected how you dealt with that," Jake said. "They started opening up to you, and I think that's when you stopped being a hard ass."

"Yeah, well, Midshipman Livingston didn't like it. He was waiting for me with a baseball bat. Can you believe that ass actually stalked me long enough to figure out my jogging patterns? Lucky for me, Jake passed me and ran across Livingston first."

"Passing you was easy," Jake said. "A turtle could have done it."

Chuckles filled the air.

"He had the bat hidden behind some vans and said he was walking off a cramp," Jake said. "Lucky I recognized him in time to turn around. Luckier still that I came back for you."

Inquisitive eyes turned to Brody. He looked at his beer and smiled.

"As Midshipman Slate was passing me, I stopped him and fried him for jogging after Taps. I was going to have him restricted to the academy for weeks. Later, when that ass jumped out from the van and whacked my shins, my first thought was that God was punishing me for punishing Jake."

"By the time I got there," Jake said, "he was huddled on the parking lot and that redneck wasn't stopping with the bat except to catch his breath."

"Not until you showed up. One second I'm getting beat, the next, Jake's throwing rocks at the guy, pissing him off, and luring him toward a van. Before you know it, Jake's on top of the van, and the stupid shit tries to follow him up with the bat. Jake swoops down and has the guy's arms behind his back in a – what is it?"

"Double arm bar," Jake said. "I wrestled in high school. Hurts like a son of a bitch."

"You also didn't mention that you were still thinking about becoming a Navy SEAL at that point."

"I was crazy back then," Jake said.

"And we decided the next morning that you would be much happier as a submarine officer," Brody said. "I consider my sage and unbiased career advice a token of my gratitude."

"Smartest move I made," Jake said.

Jake felt happy until he remembered that the career move to submarines had led him to the accident that had left the damage lurking inside him that no one else could see.

★

Two hours later, Jake stared at tortilla crumbs, empty shot glasses, and beer pitchers. A waitress cleared the mess and took an order for two more pitchers and a plate of nachos.

Feeling his mind melting into a puddle of beer and tequila, Jake drifted in and out of a conversation about hockey returning to Hartford, but he woke up at the mention of a single word.

"...*Severodvinsk*," Lieutenant Keller said.

"I read about the '*Miami-Severodvinsk* Encounter' in the top secret publications," Jake said. "I didn't expect to hear about it here."

"When you get *Miami* sailors around pitchers of beer, you're going to hear about it."

"Eighteen months ago," a bleary-eyed Brody said, "the technologically advanced superstar Russian *Severodvinsk* submarine went on its maiden deployment. So we sent the *Virginia* to spy on the bastard, but the *Virginia* had reactor problems and had to limp home on its diesel."

"The *Virginia* had reactor circuitry failure after they botched some maintenance, and that's end game for the reactor," Keller said, "but it gave us a chance to kick ass!"

"We were deployed in the Atlantic when we got the radio message to take over the hunt," Brody said. "I knew the *Severodvinsk* would be quiet, but it turns out this thing was practically a ghost.

"That *Severodvinsk* had all the newest goodies - updated hydrophone hardware and data processing. But we still kicked its butt. And I'll tell you how. We outsmarted him, and we were better trained.

"I figured the *Severodvinsk* would conduct training attacks against the *Truman* battle group that was transiting to the Mediterranean. Russians still can't resist stalking aircraft carriers. If they can still do it, they can sell the hardware and training to plenty of buyers.

"So I estimated an intercept course and waited on the Russian's track. Then I slowed the *Miami* to reduce our noise signature and to listen. I caught that *Severodvinsk* moving by us at fifteen knots."

The waitress returned with beer and nachos. Brody took a long swallow.

"We were taking in frequency data, sound power level, direction, screw blade rate and even heard his hull pop as it expanded when he ascended to periscope depth," Brody said. "We had this guy nailed.

"Then we radioed in his position. The helicopters from the *Truman* used their dipping sonar to play ping-pong with him. The Russian had to turn tail and sprint home!"

Beer glasses clanked, Jake paid the bill, and the group staggered onto the curb in search of a taxi.

During the ride home, Jake regretted that his mentor, Brody, the legend of the '*Miami-Severodvinsk* Encounter', had been passed over for promotion, reduced to heavy drinking, and now faced a failing marriage.

Everything he had believed about patriotism and the United States Navy imploded and filled him with rage. In his revenge, he would take no prisoners.

CHAPTER SIX

⊢——————————————————————————⊣

THE NEXT DAY JAKE BLEW off steam at his tai kwon do dojang studio. It was almost midnight.

He bounced on his heels. A springy carpet energized him as he envisioned a face on a kicking bag. The top of his bare foot struck padded vinyl. The thump echoed. Jake imagined his victim doubling over in pain.

He jumped back and pulled his knee to his chest. Whipping his torso toward his imaginary target, he slashed a foot across the bag. The imaginary victim dropped to a knee.

"Get up," he said.

Bouncing, Jake adjusted the black belt around his waist and pulled up the white pants of his dobak uniform.

"Get up!"

Jake's heel sent the bag into orbit. As the bag swung back, he unleashed a flurry of kicks to an imaginary jaw until he was exhausted.

Heaving and muscles burning, Jake slumped to the ground. Wheezing, he clasped his fingers atop his head and raised his rib cage to let his lungs expand. As his breathing quieted, he listened to the silence.

Glaring at the kicking bag, Jake took a last look at the target of his anger: Commander Thomas Henry, the commanding officer of the USS *Colorado*. What had happened to him had been no accident.

Jake craved revenge, but violence alone would not satisfy him. He wanted to ruin Henry without spending the rest of his life in jail and needed a better method than mock beatings to help him even the score.

★

At Jacksonville International Airport, Pierre Renard's lover and assistant, Marie Broyer, slid into the driver's seat of a rental Taurus. A few turns led her to I-95 northbound where she let cars pass as she admired the greenery lining the four-lane highway.

Educated at the Sorbonne, Marie had never done spy work, but Renard assured her that her charm and tact were sufficient qualifications. Now she would find out if he was right.

Five minutes after crossing into Georgia, Marie brought the Taurus down a subdivision's entry road, drove by small houses and arrived at 1206. She noticed a Jeep Grand Cherokee in the open garage and committed the license number to memory.

She rounded a cul-de-sac and passed the house again. She would find a hotel and sleep. At night she would return to the main road to await the Jeep. If it came, she would trail it to a bar or restaurant where she could approach the lieutenant.

Her heart skipped a beat as she glanced in her rearview mirror. The Jeep had backed out of the garage. Fearing that Slate had seen her, she accelerated.

The Grand Cherokee reached the intersection behind her but turned the other way. She circled through the gravel shoulder and followed Jake onto I-95 southbound. After twenty minutes, his right turn signal flashed. Marie smiled as she followed him, retracing her path to the airport.

She parked near Jake's Jeep and followed him on foot to the terminal. She had committed his image to memory. He had broad shoulders and a thin waist. His jaw line was strong.

A woman could not fail to recognize him, she thought.

He approached the ticket desk, and she moved closer, hoping he would stop, but instead he went straight to the security line.

Marie studied the departures. Only three flights were leaving Jacksonville within the hour – one each for New York, Chicago, and Denver – and Jake Slate looked like the type of man who wouldn't waste time playing it safe by arriving early for a later flight.

She gambled and bought a first-class ticket for a flight to Chicago that was departing in thirty minutes.

After passing through security, she looked for Jake. She had guessed right. He was waiting for the flight to O'Hare International Airport.

Exhausted from a day that had begun twenty-eight hours earlier in Paris, she boarded the 737. Once seated in a first class chair, she fell immediately asleep.

★

At the airport, Marie deplaned and waited for Jake at a magazine stand. As he approached, she lowered her face.

He passed, and she followed him through the twists and turns of O'Hare to the elevated subway. Boarding the train, she worked her way forward car by car until she found him. Then she retreated and sat one car back.

Thirty minutes later the train stopped, and Marie followed Jake onto a wooden platform and down stairs to the corner of State and Lake.

Reaching street level, she saw Jake turn east onto Lake Street, and she broke into a trot to close distance. A heel slipped out from under her, and her ankle bent over. She mumbled an obscenity, wiggled her foot, and placed weight on it.

Uninjured, she turned south onto Wabash and followed Jake underneath the inner loop where he entered a bar. Before following him in, she placed her sunglasses in her purse and checked her reflection in a bank's window.

Jake would notice her pronounced cheekbones and petulant lips. He would notice her alluring curves, too. All men did.

Confident of her seductiveness, she entered the bar, ordered a vodka martini, and worked her way around a pool table into Jake's view. His gaze flickered over her body.

Knowing she had his attention, Marie smiled, sipped from her drink, and looked away.

A booming voice from across the room startled her.

"Jake, get over here and give me a hug, buddy!"

As Jake darted toward a tall, smiling man, Marie retreated.

CHAPTER SEVEN

INHALING FROM A MARLBORO, PIERRE Renard sat in the antechamber of the Taiwanese Minister of Defense.

He had just verified the identity of the mole who had thwarted his theft of the Russian nuclear warheads. During the attempt, the Deputy Defense Minister had made a hasty departure from the island.

Renard had then proposed a new plan to enact his revenge against mainland China for his bullet wound. The Minister had agreed to it, and Renard was looking forward to an evening of pondering the details over cognac when his phone chimed.

"Hello," he said.

"Hello, my love," Marie said.

Marie had been distant from his mind. The sound of her voice excited and confused him. He had no time to sort out his feelings for Marie but doubted he could understand them if given eternity.

"How was your flight?" he asked. "Keep it sanitized. There are listening and descrambling stations in Taipei."

"I've had several flights, most recently landing in Chicago."

"It sounds like you're in a nightclub. Am I paying you to display your charms across the states?"

"No, my dear. It seems that a new interest of mine has traveled a long way this evening to visit a friend. He's quite handsome, you know."

Renard recognized one feeling for Marie - jealousy.

"Handsome? You're already enamored with him?"

"Not yet, but I cannot say how long I will be able to resist. He's seen me also, and I'm confident he was impressed."

"Then you will continue per plan?" he asked.

"Yes, but I must add that he has an attractive friend here in Chicago. I guess the handsome ones run in packs."

"Then I suppose you will enjoy seducing both men."

"I will let you use your imagination."

As Renard noticed that Marie had hung up on him, he could not tuck away thoughts of Marie preparing to seduce a man at his request. He slid the phone into his blazer.

His Marlboro became ashes, and he pressed it into an ashtray. He could not admit to himself that he loved Marie, but something within him ached. Before he could mentally tag that aching as 'loneliness', he stood and set out to design the battle plan for the Minister of Defense.

★

Jake poured a beer for the friend he had met ten years earlier in high school. Grant Mercer, a futures trader on the Chicago Board of Trade, flashed a boyish smile.

"So what's up, Jake? We haven't talked much lately."

"Got a lot on my mind, buddy."

"Let me guess. Asshole captain still on your ass?"

"He's on everyone's ass. As usual. He's like the anti-John. I wish all skippers could be like Brody."

"Your mentor?"

"Yeah."

Mercer sipped his beer.

"You seem down," he said.

"Yeah, I am. I've got a lot on my mind."

"Is it the accident?"

"Back the fuck off!" Jake said.

Mercer raised his eyebrow.

"Sorry," Jake said. "I don't want to talk. I came here so you could help me forget about it."

"Well, if you want to talk, we'll talk," Mercer said. "If not, we can run around and chase women like the mindless slaves to our penises we are."

As a result of the depression that accompanied his anger, Jake's libido had all but died since the accident.

"Maybe after a few beers," Jake said and slammed a beer. "Speaking of which, we've run out."

"Okay. Let's go," Mercer said. "We need a new scene."

★

A piercing whistle escaped from between Mercer's fingers. A cab hit a U-turn on Wabash. Deafened, Jake cast an evil eye at Mercer but caught sight of an attractive woman in her mid-thirties standing behind them. He recognized her from the bar.

The woman's curves kindled the strongest lust he had felt since his accident, and his primal sex drive seemed foreign. While Jake froze, Mercer drew Marie into a conversation.

"Hey, that's some nice accessorizing. The green and yellow pastels go well with your dark brown hair," Mercer said.

"You have a sharp eye for an American man. Either that or you're just a good bullshitter," Marie said.

"It's a little of both, actually. Hey, what's that accent? Are you French?"

"I flew in from Paris just today."

"Fantastic. Jake here speaks French," Mercer said.

Oh shit, Jake thought. *I've just forgotten every word.*

"I have yet to set my watch. *Vous avez l'heure?*" Marie asked.

"It's almost eleven," Jake said.

He thought the lady showed a little class by offering the English hint.

"If you want to hear me speak French," he said, "you're going to have to bribe me or get me really drunk."

"Neither task sounds too hard," Marie said.

"She's got you there, buddy," Mercer said. "You're an underpaid drunken sailor."

Jake stuck out a hand. *"Je m'appelle Jake."*

"Marie. *Enchantée.*"

Mercer extended his hand to finish the salutations.

"We're going to Stanley's," he said. "Care to join us?"

"Oui."

★

Stanley's, a wedge-shaped tavern on a rare Chicago diagonal street at the corner of Sedgwick and Lincoln, became a dive at night. Scattered peanut shells covered the floor. The stench of cigarettes and perfume was overwhelming, and speakers pumped out a pulsing beat.

Jake pushed to a table and ordered drinks. Marie excused herself and went to the ladies room.

"She's hot!" Mercer said over pulsating music.

"No doubt. What's she see in us?"

"A ménage à trois, of course," Mercer said and flashed the impish smile that had always made Jake laugh.

"Get serious! I think I'm in love."

"You're in lust," Mercer said.

"Maybe. But she's built, educated, and refined."

"She can't keep her eyes off you," Mercer said.

A waitress brought drinks. Jake slid a beer in front of Mercer and watched his friend scan the room.

"When she comes back," Mercer said, "I'm going to excuse myself to talk to some buddies I see across the room. After you talk a while, take her across the street to Gamekeepers. It's quieter."

Marie returned and Jake handed her a beer.

"What are you two discussing?" she asked.

"You," Mercer said.

She laughed.

"Tell me about you instead."

"The Board of Trade is a great place to get filthy rich, and I plan to stay there until I die of an ulcer. Look, you two will have to excuse me.

I see some friends, and if I don't talk to them now, they'll just barge in on us later."

Mercer walked away.

"That leaves me alone with the naval officer," Marie said and smiled.

"And it leaves me with the attractive French PhD."

"You flatter me."

"Just stating the facts, ma'am."

Jake sipped his beer. It was a local microbrew that left an aftertaste of hops.

"So, tell me what you do in the Navy," Marie said.

"Pretty much since my last year at the Academy, I've committed myself to the dream of commanding a submarine. So I became a submarine officer."

"I know a man - a close friend, actually - who commanded a French submarine."

"Do you know how much power a commanding officer has?" Jake asked.

"My friend mentioned that he missed the authority he once had."

"Did your friend ever tell you any good stories about what it's like to command?"

"He told me how he loved the power, but he also mentioned that political forces constrained him."

"True."

Marie leaned forward.

"I'm sorry, Jake. I cannot hear you."

Jake motioned that Marie should follow him out of the bar.

At Gamekeepers, Jake drank a pint of LaBatt while Marie sipped from a vodka martini. He talked about his newest hobby of rock climbing.

Marie described the beauty she had seen while hiking between the rustic towns scattered among the wooded hills of the Luberon region. Their conversation flowed for hours.

Jake had suffered weeks of poor spirits, but a beer buzz and an intriguing woman had lightened his heart.

"I would like to hear more about your career," she said.

"Well, unfortunately, I got assigned to a Trident Missile submarine with a bastard for a captain. It's been hard."

"I read Caine Mutiny. Your captain is not named Queeg, is he?" Jake smiled.

"We call him Ahab. I volunteered Bly and Queeg, but they didn't stick."

"They say that absolute power corrupts absolutely," Marie said.

"My captain proves that theory, but I also know a guy, a really good friend, who commands a submarine and is loved by his men," he said. "So maybe you can have power and keep your integrity."

"I understand that a submarine is a good place to wield power," Marie said. "But if you really want power, then why limit yourself to a submarine? You could influence more people and earn more money by running a company."

"Good point. But there's an allure to submarines that you can't find anywhere else. Picture wielding amazing destructive force in absolute secrecy."

"I doubt I would like that," Marie said. "War does not appeal to me. I can only imagine the allure."

And now, that's all I can do, he thought.

Marie's gaze became soft and inviting.

"It's late, Jake. Would you be willing to escort me to my hotel? I'm new to town, after all."

Part of him wanted to accept the invitation. Another part resisted. He decided that he would be a gentleman and escort her.

★

A cab brought Jake and Marie to the Sheraton Towers lobby. He slipped the cabbie a generous tip and led her through the lounge and back into the cool night where they stood before a wall overlooking the Chicago River.

A breeze blew and she shivered. Jake placed his arm around her. He watched with anticipation as her lips moved toward his.

"Wait!" he said and turned his head.

Marie pulled away.

"I'm sorry," he said.

"I thought you were attracted to me."

"I am."

Jake held her.

"A piece of machinery on my submarine blew up and cut me pretty badly. It left me practically impotent."

"I'm so sorry," she said. "But you're still an interesting person."

The comment lifted his spirits.

"Can I talk to you again?" he asked.

"Certainly. Why not?"

"Thanks," Jake said. "I appreciate it."

"Perhaps we can talk tomorrow. Perhaps even meet for lunch. It's your decision."

"Take a cab to Einstein Bros Bagels on Clark Street, by North Avenue. When I'm in town, Grant and I always eat there from about eleven to noon."

"I will meet you there at eleven."

CHAPTER EIGHT

POURING OVER CHARTS IN THE antechamber of the Taiwanese Minister of Defense, Renard lifted his wireless phone. He was eager to know what Marie had found.

"You've discovered something?" he asked.

"Our man claims to have recently become impotent from an accident at sea," Marie said.

"Unfortunate," Renard said but felt his lips curling into a cruel smile.

"I did not pry. But by his demeanor, I suspect neglect or even malice in the events surrounding the accident."

"Is he depressed - anxious?"

"I'm tired," she said. "It's been a long day."

"Please, I have little time."

She sighed.

"You must continue," Renard said. "You're discovering details about this man that can turn him into an ally. You might be finding something of incredible value to me."

"I thought I was of incredible value to you."

"Of course you are."

"Nice to hear it," she said.

"About our man? His state of mind?"

"He's perfectly rational and not lacking in self-confidence. In fact, I wondered at times tonight who was seducing whom."

"Must you tease me?" he asked.

"You deserve it! You use me like a whore and expect me to be your loyal handmaid?"

"Can you forgive me for the time being?"

"Perhaps."

"Thank you. About our man?"

"He rides an off-road motorcycle, practices tai kwon do, and climbs rocks," she said.

"Then he does not lack courage. Or bravado. What of his friends and family?"

"He seems to have only a few friends. He told me his father was a CIA officer who died young at the hands of the Chinese. His mother died several years ago. I did not pry for more details."

"You've done very well. Get a suite by the airport and leave word of your coordinates with my assistant in Marseille. I will meet you there as soon as I can, but I have a project here I must finish first."

"I can get more information from him before I leave."

"How is that possible?" he asked.

"I have a rendezvous with him tomorrow. I agreed to see him for lunch and coffee."

"To torment me or to help me?"

"Perhaps I did so with no regard to you whatsoever."

"You must not show. Leave Chicago tomorrow morning."

"That's cruel!" she said.

"If you fail to show, he will blame your absence on his condition and become more frustrated. I need him to feel alienation and isolation in order to exploit him."

"Do you understand anything but how to manipulate people?" Marie asked.

"I'm cursed with such a gift," Renard said. "Is our man returning home soon?"

"He was to stay here only during the weekend."

"Follow him home. I will join you in two days."

★

Through the window of Einstein Bros Bagels, Grant Mercer watched huddled pedestrians fight Chicago's wind. He slurped a latté.

The man across the table stared at a half-eaten cinnamon bagel. Mercer couldn't remember having seen his friend so despondent.

"She isn't coming," Mercer said.

Jake remained stone.

"Jake, you know the odds. It's a coin toss if you ever see a woman after the first night. It just seems worse because you thought you had a connection."

Still stone.

"Let's get out of here. Maybe we can talk about it outside," Mercer added.

On the sidewalk, Mercer zipped his Timberland jacket.

"Look, man, I know how you feel," he said.

Mercer felt himself being pulled at his shoulders and spun like a top. He flailed his arms and dug his fingers into Jake's biceps. Expecting his knees to smack the sidewalk, Mercer was surprised when Jake caught him by his jacket.

"You do not know how I feel! You don't have a fucking clue. The Navy ruined my life."

Mercer let Jake hold him.

"What the fuck do you say about that?" Jake asked.

"All I want to do is to help you."

The hold loosened as Jake's voice trailed to a whisper.

"You don't know how I feel."

Jake relaxed his grip. Mercer staggered backward and pulled Jake into a hug while stabilizing himself.

"I'm here for you, buddy," Mercer said.

Jake's chest expanded with shallow breaths. Tears filled Mercer's eyes. He remembered the day nine years ago when Jake was orphaned. It was the only time he remembered seeing Jake cry.

★

From an upstairs patio of Trolleys Food and Spirits, a favorite watering hole in St. Marys, Jake watched the sun touch the horizon

over a southern Georgian tributary of the St. Marys River. Around
him, a dozen *Colorado* shipmates gorged themselves on hot wings and
beer during a warm spring day. He poured a beer for Scott McKenzie,
the *Colorado's* adulterous mechanic.

"Done like a pro, sir," McKenzie said.

"I am a pro. Pass me some wings. I'm starved."

"I've seen you eat, sir. Just save us some. There's only fifty on that
plate."

Jake devoured three wings. The fourth slithered through the bar-
beque sauce on his fingers and hit the table. He wiped his hands and
mouth.

"You know I've talked the executive officer into transferring you off
the ship, right?" Jake asked.

"Yeah, I'm going to call my detailer to argue about it though,
because he's going to send me to Groton. It's too damn cold in Connecticut," McKenzie said.

"It's not so bad up there. Plus I can talk to the commanding officer
of the *Miami* to see if he could use you. He's my mentor."

"Yeah, well I don't want to go anywhere."

"You're not still attached to our shipmate's wife, are you?" Jake
asked.

"She still calls me. I just hang up, but I still love her," McKenzie
said.

"The stars aren't aligned on this one. If you stick around here,
you're going to slip up and get caught. Trust me. You're going to have
to start over somewhere else."

McKenzie grunted.

"Yeah. I guess you're right. I'll do like you said and just get as far
away from this mess as I can. I guess I owe you one, you know, for
talking to the executive officer for me."

Jake emptied his glass. Through the corner of his eye, he spied a
figure on the street below. A woman in a green and yellow dress stood
there. Dark hair framed a face hidden behind sunglasses.

Marie? Jake thought.

As if she had heard him, the woman looked up.

Jake pushed his way through the bar's double doors. Standing in the empty street, he watched the mystery lady glance at him before slipping under the waterfront's covered pier.

He jogged to the dock and raised his hand to shield his eyes from the sun's reflection. A silver-haired man in a gray blazer sat between him and the woman who was descending stairs at the dock's far end.

The man lowered his 'USA Today'.

"Marie will not be joining us, Lieutenant Slate."

Jake looked into eyes of blue steel. The stranger closed his newspaper and lit a Marlboro with the flame from a gold-plated lighter.

"Who are you?" Jake asked.

"Pierre Renard, your agent of revenge."

"How the hell do you know my name?"

"I know a few things about you, but I cannot say how. I asked Marie to contact you."

"You sent Marie after me? Like a spy?"

"More like a recruiter."

"Recruiter for what?"

"A project that will enable you to take revenge upon those who have wronged you."

"How did you know about...Marie told you everything?"

"I apologize for my methods, but I wanted to be sure that I could offer you what you needed before flying half way across the world to meet you."

"Meet for what? Get to the point!"

Renard exhaled smoke.

"I need your assistance in acquiring warheads from your submarine."

Jake stepped back as if Renard had shape-shifted into a rattlesnake. He pushed a hand through his hair.

"Who put that idea in your head?" Jake asked.

"You did."

"I did?"

"Yes, you all but admitted to Marie that you're in the market for revenge. And I know more than you admitted to her. I know, for example, that your commanding officer is at least partially responsible for your condition, and given the extent of your injury, I would not blame you for holding the United States Navy and its bureaucratic leadership responsible."

Jake was as shocked by the man's understanding of his state of mind as his knowledge of his secrets.

"Okay," he said. "If that were true, then so what?"

"I'm sure you've pondered taking the situation into your own hands, but you're too smart for wanton aggression. This leaves you in a quandary."

Jake said nothing.

"Take warheads from the Navy that destroyed you – that will quiet your inner demons."

He hungered to join Renard in whatever scheme he was concocting, but he wanted to test the Frenchman's sincerity.

"You're a government agent trying to entrap me. Do you think I would turn my back on my country?"

"I intend to arm Taiwan with nuclear warheads to improve their position against China," Renard said. "You can help me."

He held out an envelope.

"Ten thousand dollars. I insist. This should allay your fears that I work for your government. If I did, then I've just ruined my case with entrapment."

Jake shook his head.

"Lieutenant," Renard said, "I would not be here if I were not certain that I could help you. Our interests are aligned, and I understand you more than you may know."

"Oh yeah?"

"I can see how your patriotism has been betrayed, and I know how militaries can destroy the finest men. You see, I commanded the French nuclear submarine '*Amethyst*'."

"So you're Marie's friend."

"Yes."

"Prove that you really were a French submarine commander. Tell me where you earned your commission."

"*L'Ecole Navale* near Brest. I graduated in nineteen eighty-two with seventy-six other *Aspirants*."

"Name every class of Russian surface combatant you know. A submarine captain would still know them."

"The real Russian names or the NATO nicknames?"

"Spit it out."

"Very well. *Kresta, Kynda, Konin, Kashin, Krivak, Kara, Kirov...* that's it for the K's that I can think of off the top of my head. There was, of course, that hideous helicopter carrier *Moskva* that looked like it might capsize at any moment."

Jake nodded.

"I did a summer exchange at *L'École Navale*. Tell me about your graduation party. The one I saw made my academy's Ring Dance look like geriatric bingo."

Renard sighed.

"There was, of course, the splendid fireworks display over the harbor and young men from military academies across Europe in their finest dress uniforms. Many *Aspirants* brought their sisters, and I fell prey to the most beautiful. We met at a caviar table next to an ice sculpture of the *Jean d'Arc,* our sacred training vessel."

"I remember there was no lack of babes."

"Well, this 'babe' as you say, was indeed beautiful, and quite amazing. Considerate, intelligent, refined. We married six months after the dance. We had a son."

"Sounds like a textbook story - easily memorized."

"I prefer to forget. I returned from a deployment on the *Rubis* submarine to discover that I'd lost my new family to a drunk driver."

Renard looked at the river. The sun had set over the tree line, but its receding light cast a shadow across the Frenchman's face. Jake noticed pain that looked genuine.

"Is the inquiry over?" Renard asked.

"One last question," Jake said. "Bearing to a contact is due north. Range - ten nautical miles. You're steaming east at ten knots, the contact is steaming west at ten knots. What's the bearing rate?"

"I've not done target motion analysis for years."

"I made the numbers easy. Prove you know the formula that every submarine commander knows."

"Ten nautical miles, twenty knots across the line of sight? Roughly four degrees per minute bearing rate."

"Alright, I'll buy that you were a submarine commander, at least for now."

"Then you will accept my payment?"

Renard extended the envelope again.

"How have I earned this?"

"I'm paying for your planning. You will brainstorm possibilities, using any resources you can imagine, to acquire at least ten warheads from your ship. If you agree to share your thoughts, then meet with me at the Jacksonville Airport Hilton, room two-zero-three, within three days."

Jake took the money.

CHAPTER NINE

───────────────────────────────────

Jake knew the mysterious Frenchman had set him up and used him, but he overlooked this and focused on the promise of revenge. The Frenchman didn't grasp the full hatred Jake felt for his captain's role in the accident, but he knew enough to offer him the retaliation he desired.

Jake mulled over the words that the ex-French submarine commander had delivered convincingly.

'Using any resources you can imagine'

At three in the morning, Jake's mind raced as he sifted through the library of fantasies of destroying Commander Thomas Henry that he had created since the accident. Twisting the fantasies, splitting them, and recombining them became his evening's mental adventure.

As the sun rose, Jake had devised a final vision, and if the Frenchman had the guts and resources to commit to it, the vision would become his vengeance.

★

Sleep-deprived but enthused by his plan, Jake continued the charade he had begun after the accident that he was still a naval officer.

Wearing a khaki uniform that he wanted to burn, he spent the day teaching young *Colorado* sailors damage control techniques and depth and steering control in shore-based training facilities.

In the late afternoon, he changed into jeans and drove south. He took I-95 over the bridge into Florida and followed the familiar path to Jacksonville Airport. He parked at the hotel and found the Frenchman's room.

He knocked on the door, and when the Frenchman opened it, his eyes lit up.

"Please, come in. Would you like some cognac?" Renard asked.

"Not while talking business," Jake said.

"So you will share your ideas with me?"

"I'm not here to ask you on a date."

"Well then, as a gesture of good faith, let me pay you in advance."

"Wrong," Jake said. "Hold your money. I'm driving you somewhere."

"I will entertain your suspicions. Lead on."

"Wrong again. Strip down naked."

"Excuse me?"

"Wires and taps are my enemies tonight. I know you've been naked in front of men on a submarine, so lose the shyness. Strip down."

"Should I wiggle my ass for you?"

"Just do it."

After Jake glanced over the Frenchman's naked body and saw no wires or gadgets, he nodded toward the closet.

"Put on a new set of clothes."

Renard donned a fresh pair of Chino's and a white dress shirt. He threw his gray blazer over his shoulder and grabbed a duffel bag stuffed with hundreds.

"Okay. Let's go," Jake said.

★

At a table in an airport sports bar, Renard inhaled a fresh cigarette. Each step that Jake took in expressing interest drew him deeper into a commitment. Renard felt the steady wheels of recruitment in motion.

"I'm very curious to hear your ideas," he said.

"You can't get to the warheads unless you want to cut or blow through two inches of steel," Jake said. "That's too much noise, too much time, and too complicated. But you can have the entire ship itself."

Renard held the Marlboro away from his face while coughing.

"*Merde.* The entire ship?"

"We're scheduled for switching out a few missiles, so we'll be in the explosive handling wharf the night before patrol. It's a covered, solitary pier. You give me some commandos – Taiwanese I assume - and I can take control of the ship from the covered wharf and move it wherever you want. You interested?"

The naval officer's ambition and audacity stunned Renard, but he hid his surprise.

"Yes, of course," Renard said. "Explain your plan."

"Tell me where you want to drop off the warheads."

"I imagine that I could arrange for a transfer to a Taiwanese ship in secrecy, probably in the Pacific."

"Fine," Jake said. "I figured as much."

Jake unfolded his ideas about stealing the *Colorado*. Renard listened and contributed his ideas to fill in the few gaps that Jake had not considered. Any doubt he had about Jake's mental ability vanished as the lieutenant outlined his plans.

After half an hour, Renard had digested Jake's thoughts. He found them impressive. He flicked the gold-plated Zippo under a fresh Marlboro as Jake qualified his commitment.

"I still need to recruit my men, but the guys I have in mind will jump at it. You can consider the success of your project a foregone conclusion, provided you give me the supporting resources and offer the right price."

"I will see to your resources," Renard said. "As for your payment, the duffle bag holds fifty thousand dollars. That makes sixty thousand thus far."

"Petty cash," Jake said.

"Agreed. For a plan of the magnitude you've suggested, if you can carry it out successfully, I can offer you five million dollars."

"Do you think I can live on that forever?"

"Yes, of course."

"I want one hundred million," Jake said. "And you can call that a bargain."

Renard had hoped Jake would focus less on the money than on the revenge but appreciated his cool business head. He liked that in his recruits.

He couldn't finance the sum from his own holdings, but he trusted that the Taiwan Minister of Defense would consider it a bargain. And since he planned on negotiating his fee with the Minister as a percentage of the total price, a higher cost of business suited him.

"I will ask my clients for funding. Recruit your team, and I will return in ten days with your answer. I will send word of where to meet me."

★

Alone in his hotel, the Frenchman reflected.

His plan had taken on new life in the passion of the young naval officer, but could this be a ploy? Was the American working with authorities to entrap him?

He poured himself a Hennessy. As the drink's warmth relaxed him, he convinced himself that his fears were baseless. The situation had unfolded per his desires.

Even if Jake tried to back out or turn on him, Renard thought, he had influence with the Taiwanese Minister of Defense. He would control all Taiwanese assets involved with the theft of the *Colorado*. That would serve as an insurance policy. He would deliver warheads to Taiwan and alter the course of history.

CHAPTER TEN

MAY 7, 2006
HILTON GARDEN INN, JACKSONVILLE AIRPORT:

RENARD HAD CONVINCED THE TAIWANESE Minister of Defense to pay
Jake's one hundred million dollars in installments during the stolen
Trident's voyage. He also negotiated twenty million in commission
fees for himself.

With mainland China nearing implementation of its blockade-
reunification plan, the Minister of Defense had little strength to turn
down Renard's demand for a ten percent down payment. The Frenchman banked his two million dollar commission fee for the down payment and returned to Jacksonville, Florida.

★

The fatigue of transoceanic travel reminded Renard of the long
hours commanding the *Amethyst*. Feeling his age, he wondered if he
had enough energy to carry out the plan. He hoped that Jake would
provide a much needed spark.

He watched Jake enter his hotel room and lay an attaché case on a
table.

"I've got the drawings of the ship and the Kings Bay nautical charts," Jake said.

"Do I have to strip? I wore a thong for you."

"We're beyond that. Can you meet my terms?"

"Yes. Ten million up front. Forty million at your midway maneuver, the remaining fifty million upon delivery."

"When do I get the ten million?"

"It's in an account now. After I hand you the account number and access code, the money is yours. However, once you change the code, you're committed. If you run with the money, you will be hunted down and killed."

"I'm going through with this as long as you remember whose ship it is," Jake said. "The warheads are yours, but the ship is mine. Even after the warhead transfer, it's mine. I'll need it to get away."

"The ship itself is only a delivery vehicle to me."

"So we agree. I'm in command?"

"Yes, of course."

"Good. I don't want to have this conversation when we're at sea. I know the ship much better than you ever will, and I have a few tricks up my sleeve if you test me."

"It will be a twenty-year step backward, but I must concede command. You know the *Colorado* much better than I do, and you also know the men you've recruited. I assume you've recruited them?"

"I talked to them a few days ago. They're with us."

Renard wanted to learn what he could about Jake's men.

"Tell me about them," he said.

"First guy is Machinist Mate Second Class Scott McKenzie, a crack mechanic. He can operate or repair any non-nuclear system on the boat. He ran into a little trouble with someone else's wife. I'd planned to get him transferred, but his ten million cut changed that."

"Ten million?" Renard asked. "You're giving each of your men ten percent and keeping seventy for yourself?"

"Keeping fifty. I have a land-based guy taking another twenty percent."

Renard believed that the way one deals with money reveals much about one's character.

"It may be none of my business how you share your funds, but I appreciate your candor," he said. "And of the other two who will deploy with us?"

"The Navy was a mistake for both, and they want out. They hate their jobs and they're both in debt up to their eyeballs. Electrician's Mate Third Class David Bass is McKenzie's counterpart in the electric world, plus he's qualified to handle most reactor control stations. He needs the money to help save his family's business."

"And the third man?"

"Machinist Mate Second Class Michael Gant is the expert on reactor mechanical systems. He's greedy, and he lost everything in the stock market. He started drooling when I mentioned the money. All three of my guys are friends. They helped talk each other into it."

"Their qualifications and motivations seem appropriate. I have no choice but to trust your judgment about their loyalty."

"No, you don't," Jake said.

"Shall we review the details one last time then?"

"The *Colorado* just moved to the explosive handling wharf," Jake said. "Our timeframe is still good."

"Excellent. Humor me with a final walk through."

After listening to the tight chain of events that were to culminate in the theft of the *Colorado*, Renard watched Jake move toward the door. He surveyed Jake's body language. He moved fluidly and appeared relaxed. His gaze was neutral, neither afraid nor filled with bravado. Renard liked what he saw.

"So that's it," Jake said. "Next time I see you, you're wearing a wetsuit. This is your last chance to ask for anything."

"Ah, yes. Your ship does not permit smoking, does it?"

"No, but some guys carry cigarettes for port calls."

"Just in case - could you smuggle aboard a carton of Marlboros?"

"Only one carton?"

"Make it two," Renard said. "Just to be sure."

Jake grabbed a black and teal Jacksonville Jaguars football gym bag. Silencers for M-16 military rifles and nine-millimeter pistols clanked. Renard noticed a wry smile.

"I don't suppose you're going to tell me where you got these?" Jake asked.

"Just make sure you smuggle them onto the ship. And do not forget my Marlboros, or I shall be an unpleasant shipmate."

★

Alone at the dojang studio, Jake bounced on his heels. He stood before the kicking bag and envisioned a crippled Commander Thomas Henry lying before him.

He controlled his breath after having mock-pummeled Henry, adjusted the black belt around his waist, and pulled up the white pants of his dobak martial arts uniform.

Jake let the imaginary Henry stand again for another whipping. The top of his bare foot struck padded vinyl, and as the thump echoed, Jake felt his anger subside.

A sensation he had not felt in weeks came over him. He felt peace. He envisioned a Frenchman with a cigarette in his mouth promising that revenge would be his.

He drove home, showered, and slept soundly for the first time since the accident.

★

The next evening, moonlight beamed through Jake's riding goggles. He straddled the leather seat of his Kawasaki KX-500 two-stroke dirt bike. His irises expanded as he stared at the ramp's silhouette. Bending forward, he gunned the green monster's single piston engine.

He kicked the gear shifter and released the clutch. The drive train engaged, and the chain snapped. Jake ripped the bike through second gear and kicked it into third.

The bike's rpm hit the stratosphere as the ramp smacked the knobby front tire. Jake reached an unprecedented height. He tried to gage his landing but saw only darkness. Instinct alone governed his landing.

The ground surprised him, riveted foot pedals into his boots, and slammed the handlebars into his wrists. The bouncing Kawasaki tried to buck him, but he held.

Jake inhaled and brought frozen lungs back to life. He relaxed his arms as the Kawasaki came to rest.

Cutting the ignition, Jake hopped off the machine. Letting the bike fall, he ripped the chinstrap from his neck, hurled his helmet into the sky, and raised his index fingers to the night.

His ideals shattered, Jake would follow nobody else's rules and would risk everything for his revenge. He knew he was capable of pulling it off.

But unlike jumping his dirt bike, there would be no second chances.

CHAPTER ELEVEN

WARM WIND CARESSED RENARD'S CHEEKS as he glanced over the bow of a leisure craft. He aimed a flashlight into the St. Marys River, illuminating reeds at the water's edge. A sign jutting from the tranquil surface warned unauthorized craft to turn back from government property. Renard lowered the light, cut the craft's engine, and drifted into a cove.

Six men in wetsuits sprang from the leisure craft's cabin. They teamed up to inspect and adjust each other's scuba gear and slipped into the water. One of them, Sergeant Kao Yat-sen, a veteran Taiwanese commando, stayed behind with Renard.

Renard felt Kao tugging on his scuba equipment.

"Your equipment is properly fastened," Kao said. "After you are in the water, grab the strap across Mister Tiger's back. He is our strongest swimmer."

Pulse racing, Renard watched polymer hoods bob in shimmering moonlight. A raised thumb broached near a head, indicating that a young commando, mission-named Tiger, waited to help him swim to the *Colorado*.

Renard bit his mouthpiece and inhaled stale air from his rebreather. He leapt flippers-first over the side. Coolness enveloped him.

A gloved hand pulled his wrist and guided his grip to a web belt. His escort commando turned, and the belt jerked his arm. He twisted to his stomach and kicked to keep pace with his escort to the *Colorado*.

★

Palms sweating, Jake hung up a phone in the *Colorado's* control room. He had just broken Renard's ten million dollar account into a seven million dollar account for himself and Mercer and three one million dollar accounts for his hijack accomplices.

He glanced around the empty room and tapped at the phone again.

"Hello?" Grant Mercer asked.

Realizing that failure to steal the *Colorado* would make this the last conversation with his friend, Jake froze.

"Hello!" Mercer said.

"It's a go," Jake said.

Jake had offered Mercer twenty percent of the theft's price in exchange for controlling the money and a pivotal shore-based role.

Telling his friend the heist had begun, Jake expected that Mercer would call his bank and change the access code on his seven million dollar account. Then he would move his two million dollar share into his personal account before fleeing Chicago, leaving Jake with five million.

"It's a go, here. Good luck," Mercer said.

Jake hung up and dialed again. In the *Colorado's* engine room, more than a football field away, Machinist Mate Second Class Mike Gant answered.

"Yeah?"

"Petty Officer Gant, I just called the bank. You, Bass, and McKenzie are rich."

"Serious?"

"You didn't forget your access code, did you?"

"No."

"Then make a telephone call and tell me if I'm serious. You have twenty minutes before I run the drill."

★

Jake tossed a key, a training prop with a red tag hanging from it that read 'Captain's Firing Key', onto the linoleum deck. He raised a microphone to his mouth. His voice resonated throughout the ship.

"Security violation in the control room," he said. "A classified key was found on the deck. Security alert team, lay to the control room. Back up alert team, report to the forward small-arms locker. Security violation in the control room."

Jake twisted a metal handle. The pulsating siren of the general alarm rang throughout the *Colorado.* Half a minute later, he told his red-eyed duty crew that the violation was a drill.

Rubbing sleep from their eyes, sailors teamed up in pairs with unloaded weapons, searched for intruders, scanned for bombs, and simulated a communications network with squadron personnel.

After thirty minutes, Jake ordered his duty crew to assemble in the crew's mess and wait for a debriefing while he completed his midnight tour of the ship.

★

The explosive handling wharf, covered by a hangar to hide submarine missile and torpedo movements, kept the *Colorado* invisible to the outside world. Lights nestled six stories high between the rails of an overhead crane network bathed the covered wharf in yellow.

Jake found the buzz and glow within the hangar surreal, but the sweet scent of algae rising from stagnant saltwater reminded him that he stood upon the back of a real submarine.

He strained his eyes for signs of uninvited life in the dark silence outside the hangar. Confident that no unexpected visitors spied upon him from outside the covered wharf, he inspected the nylon lines that held the *Colorado* to the pier.

The lines swung low, as did the sprawl of cables, ropes, and piping that mated the submarine to shore facilities. The *Colorado's* life support was in place.

Jake approached the ship's conning sail, a tower rising from the front of the boat out of which extended fairwater planes that resembled undersized wings and served the purpose of fine-tuning the *Colorado's* depth.

Beside the sail stood a rotund young man with a twelve-gauge shotgun slung across his back.

"What's up, sir? Taking your midnight tour of this old steel pig?"

"That's right, Heitzman," Jake said.

Jake glanced over his shoulder. From the engine room, Scott McKenzie climbed through a hatch carrying a tool bag. Jake looked back at Heitzman who, accustomed to machinist mate mechanics working all hours, ignored McKenzie.

Jake scanned the water. He saw no sign of Renard or Taiwanese commandos, but he sensed they were there.

"Heitzman, you're the topside sentry, right?"

"Yes, sir."

"Where's the topside petty officer?"

"Davis is...let's see."

Jake followed Heitzman behind the sail to join the topside petty officer. Petty Officer Davis leaned against the sail under a fairwater plane, his arms crossed while staring at the hangar's far side concrete peninsula.

"Mister Slate, I swear I saw something under that pier over there," Davis said in a southern drawl. "Something kicked up water."

"How many fish have you seen popping up around here, Davis? And how about the dolphins? You wouldn't shoot Flipper between the eyes, would you?" Jake asked.

"I guess you're right, sir. I must sound like a paranoid bastard, but I just got a funny feeling."

"Everyone gets funny feelings before spending two and a half months underwater," Jake said. "It's okay."

With his sentries standing together, Jake reached for his dark blue *Colorado* ball cap. Certain that the commandos were watching, he tugged the rim and held his breath.

Two finned darts whipped through the muggy air and pierced the uniforms of both Davis and Heitzman.

Jake grabbed Heitzman's wrist with one hand, his triceps with the other, and yanked the sailor's drugged body against the sail. As Heitzman landed on the deck, Jake propelled himself toward Davis.

Davis slumped wide-eyed against the sail. He reached at the dart in his chest, but his arms fell, his eyes rolled back in his head, and he tumbled headfirst toward the basin.

Jake grasped the back of Davis' crackerjack jumpsuit and wiggled for leverage. Losing the battle against gravity, Jake reached for the sail but found only a flat wall. He looked over his shoulder at the limp sailor's body and the muddy basin seven feet below.

A chill went up his spine. A shipmate, a husband, and a father of two children would drown if he let go. Jake redoubled his efforts, swearing to himself he would not begin his journey by killing an American sailor. He yanked Davis back.

Jake stepped over the drugged sailors and studied the briny water. Five humps appeared on the surface. Near the aft of the ship, two more men swam toward the *Colorado*.

Five hooded heads broached. Facemasks covered each pair of eyes, and rubber air tubes dangled from each mouth. The mouth belonging to Pierre Renard opened, and a LAR-V rebreather mouthpiece fell to the water.

"The infiltration team is present and ready," Renard said.

"I ran the security violation drill," Jake said. "The crew is on the mess deck below. Send your team to the shore power cables and wait for my signal."

A thumb broke the water's surface and the heads again submerged.

As Renard and the commandos climbed on the wharf and submarine, Scott McKenzie came into Jake's view. The mechanic's brown eyes opened widely.

"They're here?" McKenzie asked.

He looked spooked.

"Get used it," Jake said. "This is what we all wanted. Think of the money. Think of your future. You'll have the entire world to find a new love of your life."

McKenzie froze. Jake shook him.

"Come on! Wake up! Tell me what's going on," Jake said.

"I disconnected the ship internally from shore water, air, and sewage," McKenzie said. "All I've got left is to unrig the connections topside."

McKenzie's hands were shaking.

"Everything's okay," Jake said. "Finish unrigging topside. We'll be fine."

"Unrig topside connections, aye, sir."

"You going to be okay?" Jake asked.

"I don't know about this."

"Hang with me. It's too late to turn back."

CHAPTER TWELVE

————————————————————————

A S HIS INFILTRATION TEAM HAD stormed the *Colorado,* Jake's confidence grew. The reactor startup, the crew lockdown, and the commando insertion had unfolded per plan.

Jake reached overhead and yanked a metal ring that encircled the port periscope. Hydraulic fluid hammered through pipes. The silver, oil-coated tube slithered upward. Kao stood beside him.

"When you're not handling communications for me, I'll need you looking around on the scope," Jake said.

He snapped down two black handles, pushing one and pulling the other to swivel the periscope's optics. Then he rolled the handle grips.

"This one controls elevation angle. The other switches magnification between low and high."

Jake pulled back and gestured at the optics. Kao stuck his eye to the eyepiece and fumbled with the handles.

"You got it?" Jake asked.

Kao nodded.

Jake knelt by a cubbyhole, uncoiled tangled cables, and emerged with a headset, microphone, and phone cord.

After screwing a brass connection into a ship's communication circuit, he slung a coiled cord over his shoulder, donned the headset, and depressed a button on the mouthpiece.

"Maneuvering, control room, test the sound-powered circuit," Jake said.

"Control room, maneuvering, test satisfactory," Bass said.

"Maneuvering, control room, I'm on my way to the bridge. I want the emergency propulsion motor ready to propel us out of here before I get there."

Jake slung a binocular neck strap over his head. Dangling the phone cord, he climbed three stories worth of ladder rungs through the musty and salty confines of the sail.

A steel girder floor creaked and banged against its hinges as Jake climbed into the eerie yellow hue of the explosive handling wharf. Standing on the bridge, a pit at the top of the sail, he yanked the phone cord's slack and pinched it under the girder floor.

Atop the submarine, Jake reflected that the *Colorado* was his.

★

Having seen fingers ripped off a man's hand, Scott McKenzie respected nylon lines. He mouthed warnings while draping a line in a figure eight around a cleat and kicking the rope tight against the divot.

"There," he said. "Now you try it. Here are your gloves."

A commando unraveled the line and began draping a new figure eight around the cleat.

McKenzie contemplated that spending weeks underwater with the foreign commando could be unpleasant. He tested his demeanor with small talk.

"So," McKenzie said. "Your mission name is 'Mister Tiger'. Mister Slate said you would know our names but we weren't allowed to know yours."

Tiger stepped back from his figure eight.

"Not bad," McKenzie said.

The commando placed his rifle to the deck, tied the line around his waist, and thrust lengths of nylon into the water. Tiger now stood at the submarine's edge.

"My name is to remain a secret," he said.

"Are you the tiger because you're the biggest?" McKenzie asked. "It makes sense. Mister Cheetah is the smallest, and Mister Lion looks like the guy in charge, or at least the most experienced."

"Maybe. Who cares? Your name will be in the newspaper tomorrow but mine won't."

McKenzie wanted to add something, but Tiger jumped into the basin.

Dripping, the commando reemerged on the far pier's ladder. McKenzie watched him strain while lugging the line's water-logged mass to his feet.

Muscles bulging under his black wetsuit, Tiger draped the line around the cleat twice in a figure eight. He gave McKenzie a thumbs up.

McKenzie returned the gesture, turned, and repeated the thumbs up to Jake who watched from two stories above.

★

Jake raised his sound-powered phone's mouthpiece.

"Propulsion motor, bridge, all ahead one third," he said.

"All ahead one third, aye, sir," Bass said.

Water churned behind the *Colorado*. Jake cracked a sardonic smile as his two billion dollar instrument of vengeance inched forward.

The ship protested and stopped, and Jake realized that a stabilizer, a vertical wall below the waterline, had met the pier's rubber bumper.

He raised his mouthpiece and contacted Kao in the control room.

"Mister Lion, right full rudder," he said.

"Full rudder? The display shows degrees," Kao said.

"Twenty-five degrees."

"We are turning the rudder now."

Jake watched the three-story tall rudder rotate, and the boat's tail glided away from the pier.

While the *Colorado* glided, the girder walkway brow to the pier popped free from the submarine's back. The brow skipped as the submarine crawled underneath it. Bolts snapped and yielded the walkway to the whirlpools forming beside the pier.

"Mister Lion, report ship's speed. It's a digital display to your right," Jake said.

"Speed is two point six knots," Kao said. "Mister Renard is here with me now."

"I need Mister Renard to raise the other periscope," Jake said. "I want him to visually fix our position as we navigate the channel. Landmarks are circled in red on the chart."

The starboard periscope ascended behind Jake.

"Propulsion motor, bridge, make turns for two point six knots," he said.

As the *Colorado*'s bow jutted from the covered wharf's canopy, the eerie yellow gave way to stars painted on blackness. As Jake's eyes adjusted, he noticed that the front of the submarine had veered toward the pier.

He reached for the mouthpiece jutting up from the sound-powered phone's chest plate but realized he needed the wireless unit at his hip to contact McKenzie, who roamed atop the ship's missile deck. As he fumbled to lift the unit from his hip, Jake realized he could use the sound-powered phone, undetectable outside the *Colorado*, for all communications after McKenzie returned below.

"McKenzie, hold line eight," he said.

"Hold line eight, aye, sir," McKenzie said.

Jake watched McKenzie yell to Tiger, who used the friction of figure eight turns to fight the *Colorado*. Arms bulged under Tiger's black wetsuit, and water wrung from the nylon line.

The commando played tug-of-war with the *Colorado*'s sideways momentum, the mooring line acting as a fulcrum to rotate the submarine seaward.

Its bow edging away from the pier, the *Colorado* crawled toward the open river basin. Jake aimed the ship between Crab Island, a mound of dredged silt, and the covered wharf's empty mirror image three hundred yards ahead.

"Mister Lion, rudder amidships."

"Rudder mid...I do not understand."

"Let go of it. Now!"

The rudder glided in line with the ship.

"McKenzie, take in line eight."

"Take in line eight, aye, sir"

McKenzie drew his hand across his neck. Tiger unraveled the figure eight and the *Colorado* dragged the rest of the line from the pier's cleat.

As the rope spat water, Jake watched the commando follow it into the basin. Now that he had control of the submarine, Jake wasn't sure that he cared if the commando boarded the submarine again or was left behind, but Tiger pulled on the rope and kicked his way to the tapered tail of the creeping vessel.

The first of the river's five illuminated ranges, pairs of sticks that marked the center of a channel, came into view. The range sticking up from Crab Island marked the *Colorado*'s first leg toward the sea.

A mile behind, the *Nebraska* was a blurry shadow. Jake knew that in the darkness, the *Colorado* remained invisible.

Tiger, the huskiest and now wettest commando, descended the ladder into the engine room and sealed the lower hatch with a clunk. He spied the blue dungarees of Michael Gant bent over a forest of valves, reached over his back for his rifle, and pointed it at Gant.

"Who are you?"

"Gant. I'm Michael Gant!" he said.

"Where is the injured man?"

Gant pointed, and Tiger walked to maneuvering, the engine room's control room.

Tiger hoisted Dowd's wrapped body over his broad shoulder. He then carried the unconscious sailor out of the engine room, up the missile compartment hatches, and lay him topside. Climbing back into the missile compartment, he found life vests in overhead compartments and threw them into a pile.

★

"Propulsion motor, bridge," Jake said, "shift propulsion to the port main engine. Forget the warm up. It can survive one cold iron start-up."

Water churned behind the *Colorado* as evidence that vapor hot enough to melt human bone inundated the port main engine steam turbine. The breeze caused by the *Colorado*'s nearly doubled speed fanned Jake with humid air.

"Mister Lion, right full rudder. Steady course one-five-two," Jake said.

With novice drivers, the ship turned as if driving on ice. The bow swung far right, but the Taiwanese commandos proved attentive.

"We have overshot our course," Kao said. "Mister Renard recommends from his chart that we turn left."

Jake glanced back at the range markers. Five degrees separated the upper and lower lighted sticks, indicating that the *Colorado* had drifted toward shoal water.

"Left ten degrees rudder, steady course one-four-seven."

The *Colorado* inched back into the channel as it rounded a bend, but the turn revealed the USS *Miami* at the visiting submarine pier.

Jake had forgotten that the *Miami*'s berth held a narrow but clear view of the channel. He lifted binoculars to his eyes and spied the *Miami*'s two topside sentries standing under incandescent lighting.

The *Miami*'s sentries were watching three off-duty sailors staggering on the pier. The inebriated trio teetered and bounced off each other as they sauntered along the concrete. Jake saw the drunkards hollering, but they were as inaudible as mimes. They distracted the sentries as Jake slipped the *Colorado* by the *Miami* unnoticed.

Realizing he was holding his breath, Jake exhaled. As awareness replaced his fear of being discovered, he recognized Kao's voice in his earpiece.

"Mister Slate," Kao said. "Mister Renard holds you left of track."

Jake returned his attention to navigation. He snapped his head forward as the *Colorado*'s bow pointed at a red flashing light atop a buoy that marked the channel's left side. He cringed as the buoy's tethering chain rumbled across the *Colorado*'s hull and realized he had to react before the chain snared the Trident by its stabilizer.

"Left full rudder. Back emergency. Give me everything you've got. Now!"

Water churned behind the rudder as it twisted and pulled the submarine's tail and its port stabilizer beyond the reach of the chain. Although the rudder drew the submarine from the chain, it steepened its angle toward the islands confining the channel's outer fringe. The rumbling stopped, but the ship drifted toward shoal water.

"I need a visual fix," Jake said.

Jake watched the periscope behind him swivel toward the taller light of the nearest range. The periscope swiveled again to the edge of an island and then to a distant range marker. The ex-commander of the *Amethyst* captured the fastest triangular fix Jake had seen.

Renard's voice crackled through speakers that felt like muffs over Jake's ears. He didn't trust the Frenchman yet, but he welcomed his nautical advice.

"We have shoal in front of us and on either side," Renard said. "We cannot turn. We must back out."

"I've got a backing bell on," Jake said.

"We have less than seventy yards to our stern."

"That's tight, but I can handle it," Jake said.

"A submarine of this size backing down on the surface?" Renard asked. "It will have a mind of its own. How can you be so confident?"

"Check the current in the channel," Jake said.

"Ah," Renard said. "Pushing against us. It should help straighten us out and reorient us in the channel. Your rudder and engine commands should work."

Shaken by the *Miami*, the buoy chain, and the shoals, Jake had paid no attention to which way the current was flowing. But by faking confidence, he had garnered the advice he needed and had looked strong.

"Just a scare," he said. "Everything's okay."

★

Surviving in the Chicago Board of Trade war zone took a combination of killer instincts and analytical control. By making million dollar trades, Grant Mercer had learned to replace his heart with an ice water pump.

After Jake's phone call, he had moved millions of dollars from a payphone outside his Chicago apartment. His two million was in one account and Jake's five million in another.

Not caring if his withdrawal drew attention, he forewarned his bank and took out two hundred thousand dollars in cash and stuffed it into a duffel bag for his flight through Canada.

Wearing leather gloves, Mercer grabbed the wheel of the used Honda he had bought with cash. He turned on the ice water pump in his chest, shifted the Accord into first gear, and watched his past vanish in the rearview mirror.

CHAPTER THIRTEEN

T HE REACTOR HAD REACHED CRITICALITY. White water over its bow, the *Colorado* glided through Cumberland Sound under a cloudless sky. For Jake, anticipation and fear gave way to confidence.

He took in his surroundings. To the left of the moonlit St. Marys River was the desolate southwestern tip of Georgia's Cumberland Island. To his right, the lights of Fernandina Beach, Florida, glowed on the horizon.

"Sir," Bass said, "steaming both sides of the engine room, ready to answer all bells. The electric plant is in a half-power line up on the port turbine generator."

"Shift to fast speed reactor coolant pumps," Jake said, "all ahead flank."

Jake knew that within the engine room, Bass was spinning a chrome-plated oversized steering wheel throttle and inundating the main engines with steam. The extra straining of the steam turbines would squeeze out only an extra few knots of speed, but every knot counted.

He made two turns through the channel that pointed the *Colorado* eastward, passing the stone buttresses of historical Fort Clinch on the northern tip of Florida's Amelia Island.

The *Colorado* squeezed through the narrow passage between Georgia's Cumberland Island and Amelia Island. Half a mile later, stone jetty walls, erected to protect vessels from currents, jutted through the water.

"Mister Lion," Jake said, "take the helm from Mister Cheetah and order the crew's evacuation."

"I have the helm," Kao said. "My team is positioning for the evacuation."

"I want to talk to Mister Renard," Jake said. "Have him report a visual fix."

"I hold us a half mile beyond the jetties," Renard said.

"Good," Jake said. "Not even the strongest swimmer could reach civilization before we submerge."

"I agree. It would be impossible," Renard said.

"Very well, release the crew," Jake said.

Jake watched the duty crew assemble topside.

"The entire crew is topside. Mister Cheetah is back in the control room with me," Kao said.

"Mister Lion, have Mister Tiger inform the crew that I will stop the shaft for twenty seconds," Jake said.

Jake looked over his shoulder. Tiger shut the hatch and left the *Colorado*'s duty crew to its fate. Jake ordered the shaft stopped, and turbulence behind the ship subsided.

After a moment of trepidation, one man braved the leap. Courage spread, and the entire crew jumped. Two men jumped together with a wrapped Dowd in their arms. When the last bobbing head floated into the darkness, Jake returned the ship to all ahead flank.

The *Colorado* lurched forward. One hour and forty-five minutes had passed since the heist began, and the plan was on track. Jake gave himself a cautious and silent congratulation.

West of Cumberland Island, the trawler, *Tiger Lily*, floated at anchor in a fishing haven. Michael O'Neil, a plump man with a bulbous pockmarked nose, slept in his captain's chair as a cool breeze tickled his graying beard.

He awoke, glanced at the half-empty fifth of Canadian Club whiskey he had sipped before his fitful slumber, and studied white anchor lights to check his neighbors' moorings. Then he sniffed the sweet salt air. Finally, he walked behind his pilothouse to make one last inspection of his nets and rigging before heading below.

East of the jetties, a dark mass that he recognized as the deceptively small black form of a surfaced Trident submarine raced across the water's surface. O'Neil knew how to spot Tridents and avoid them, but he had never seen one outbound at night.

He returned to the pilot house and grabbed his radio.

★

President Lance Ryder would not earn a second glance in a crowded room. His nose was too big. Although in his mid-fifties, his hairline had been receding toward a balding crown for decades. When speaking, his voice issued from thin lips tightened by deep thought.

Ryder was a war hero. While he was flying over Vietnam, flack had cut through his leg, costing him years of knee rehabilitation and giving him a limp. The old battlefield injury gave the nation confidence that his military decisions were grounded in reality.

At three forty in the morning, an aide awoke Ryder and informed him of a Broken Arrow, the theft of American nuclear weapons.

Ryder ordered the aide to have his top naval admiral contact him. As he slid into the clothes he had worn the prior day, his hopes of awaking from the nightmare dwindled. An encrypted telephone rang by his bedside.

"Ryder," he said.

Admiral Mesher, the Chief of Naval Operations and a no-nonsense submarine officer, was on the line.

"Mister President, this is the CNO. A Trident submarine is in egress from Kings Bay, Georgia, under control of an unknown force."

"How did that happen?"

"We don't know yet, sir. The USS *Colorado* was spotted forty minutes ago by a fisherman. We have no visual on its present location, but we assume it's heading east with intent to submerge. If we act quickly we can contain this."

"What do you mean 'if'? A Trident submarine can't actually slip from our grasp."

"It's possible if we can't stop it before it submerges. We have an hour. I've already ordered every anti-submarine warfare asset on the east coast into motion. I've also asked the other force commanders to help me scramble every airborne gunship-"

"Hell, no! The last thing we need is for the entire world to know we've lost a Trident."

Ryder rubbed his hand against his forehead.

"You said we have an hour," Ryder said. "Just send what you need to stop her. Don't turn this into a fleet exercise and a public relations disaster."

"I need to catch her before she can submerge."

"I got that part! What do you need from me?"

"I need control of any air asset that can be airborne, armed, and over the *Colorado* within forty-five minutes," Mesher said. "There's no telling which assets will be scrambled first, but if it's not Navy, I don't want to fight red tape getting it under my command."

"I'll make this easy for you. You can have assets in the area in two minutes. Use NORAD jets. Launch two alert aircraft and bump up the backup aircraft to the runway."

"NORAD armaments may not be enough, sir."

"Damn it, Admiral, I was an aviator. I know you can't stop a major warship with an anti-air load out. But surely you can do something with a pair of fighter jets? You can damage the rudder, can't you?"

"Yes, sir, we could certainly cripple the *Colorado* so that it can't submerge."

"Do it, then."

Ryder waited for Mesher to relay the order.

"The NORAD assets are taking off now, sir."

"Someone has taken our most potent weapon system, Admiral. I want it back and I want to know who did this."

"Yes, sir. I'll take care of it."

"If not, I'll have your balls on a silver platter."

CHAPTER FOURTEEN

JAKE DESCENDED INTO THE CONTROL room. He glanced at Scott McKenzie who was seated at the ship's control panel with his index fingers holding up silvery knobs.

"How's our weight?" Jake asked.

"I drained the hovering tanks. I'm using high-pressure air to blow the missile compensation tanks dry now. We might be too light to submerge."

"That's okay. Better light than heavy for this dive."

Jake looked around the control room. Except for Bass and Gant who remained in the engine room, the entire hijack team had assembled in the control room. Six commandos, McKenzie, and the Frenchman faced him.

"Nicely done, Mister Slate," Renard said. "The ship is yours."

Jake appreciated the vote of confidence, but he was wary. He didn't trust the hijackers, and the *Colorado* was still surfaced and vulnerable.

"Mister Slate," Kao said while removing his eye from the periscope. "We await your instructions."

"Start by taking off your masks and sunglasses," Jake said. "The crew is gone. It's just us now."

★

As the tip of the North American Air Defense's sword, Air Force Major Jeffrey Layne considered himself an elite pilot. Sitting in a cockpit on a runway at Tyndall Air Force Base, Florida, he prepared for a mission he could not believe real.

As the single Pratt and Whitney F100-PW-229 turbofan engine hummed to speed, Layne double-checked the straps that held him in the reclined pilot seat of his F-16 Fighting Falcon.

Minutes later, his helmet pressed into his headrest as the jet accelerated to Mach 2 over the eastern seaboard. A radio message confirmed that his partner, Air Force Captain Jerry Mansen, had taken position behind him.

Layne tried to imagine an enemy shrewd enough to steal a Trident. He wondered if such an enemy had the foresight to bring shoulder-launched anti-air missiles to turn a turkey-shoot into a battle.

★

Standing by a nautical chart, Jake matched the coordinates calculated by the *Colorado's* twin gyroscopic navigators against the visual data Renard had gleaned from landmarks. The coordinates from both sources agreed that charted water depth was fifteen fathoms - ninety feet.

"Mister Slate," Renard said, "you mentioned that the ship's height from keel to sail is sixty-eight feet?"

"That gives us twenty-two feet of gravy when we dive."

"*Mon Dieu!*" Renard said. "I know you planned for a shallow dive, but I thought that was for an emergency. We've escaped without notice. Surely you can wait."

"We're hours from the continental shelf," Jake said. "I don't want to wait."

"But even ten more feet could make the difference between grounding or not," Renard said.

"I don't like being surfaced, even in the dark. And the sun will rise before we reach the shelf. Scraping bottom is a risk I'm willing to take to get this pig under. I've ordered Bass to slow the ship in case we hit."

"I trust that this ship is strong and that the bottom is soft, *mon ami*," the Frenchman said.

"Everyone hold on," Jake said. "McKenzie, submerge the ship."

Jake heard clicks as McKenzie flipped six switches upward. The ship's control panel, a complex array of knobs and switches that manipulated the submarine's tanks, trim pumps, and ballast, backlit McKenzie with its glowing red indication lights. Pale skinned, McKenzie appeared ghastly as the control panel's blackness swallowed him.

"Vents are open," McKenzie said.

Jake glued his eyeball to the periscope lens and watched spray from the forward ballast tank dance in the moonlight as water spurted from the ballast tank vents. He turned and watched the after tanks vent.

The ocean crawled up the back of the ship.

★

Major Jeffrey Layne flew over an estimated position of the *Colorado*. In the receding morning darkness, he relied upon the Fighting Falcon's advanced Hughes APG-68 radar to snap up the *Colorado*'s sail.

On the fourth southward pass, Layne's heads-up display indicated that the radar had snagged a target. With civilian craft dotting the Jacksonville shipping areas, Layne needed a visual verification before launching weapons. He alerted Mansen, his wingman.

"Jerry, I've got something. Bearing one-niner-six."

"I just got it, too."

"Let's check it out."

As he dived and leveled, Major Layne examined the panorama below his cockpit. He felt so close to the ocean that he could taste salt water.

Aided by night vision, he picked up the tiny rectangular form of the *Colorado*'s semi-submerged sail and made out the slim appendage of the periscope.

"Jerry! Bearing two-zero-one."

"I see it. Doesn't look right, though. Something's out of whack."

Layne closed within one mile of the *Colorado* and examined its silhouette. Everything but the highest piece of the *Colorado* was hidden below the surface of the Atlantic. He saw only the sail.

"That's him," Layne said.

"We can't hit his rudder or screw. What do we do?"

"Let's hit the sail. It's all we've got. Follow me in!"

Layne angled his Fighting Falcon and let loose twenty-millimeter rounds.

Bullets cut through the *Colorado*'s left fairwater plane and riveted a skew line up the sail. Layne flew over the Trident and heard Mansen strafing the *Colorado* behind him.

"Jerry, open range and come about behind me. We're going to get some AMRAAMs off and make this count."

★

Chainsaw gunfire hammered through the control room.

"What the fuck was that?" McKenzie asked.

Jake recognized the high-speed repetition of bullets ricocheting through the *Colorado*'s sail as jet engines roared overhead.

"We're under attack by aircraft! Flood hovering tanks completely, flood fifty grand into both missile compensation tanks. Flood the centerline tank. Get this pig under!"

"I don't have enough hands," McKenzie said.

"I'll help," Jake said. "Mister Renard, finish lowering the scope. Everyone else hold on!"

Jake joined McKenzie at the ship's control panel.

"Ten degrees down on the stern planes," Jake said.

Tiger pushed his yoke toward the ground, activating an electro-hydraulic signal to the stern plane's hydraulic ram. At the *Colorado*'s tail, the stern planes tilted up ten degrees to drive the nose down.

Jake heard Kao call off numbers from the depth gauge.

"Eighty feet, eighty-five, ninety-"

A scraping noise filled the room as the bow hit the ocean floor.

Jake's stomach sank as the *Colorado* rebounded to the surface.

Major Layne focused on the GEC Avionics hologram Heads-Up Display that cut the darkness outside his F-16. The HUD told him that the Fighting Falcon's radar had shifted from search to fire control mode. He held missile lock on the sail and flipped a plastic guard from his trigger.

Layne's lungs froze as the Advanced Medium Range Anti-Air Missile detached from under his left wing. White flame sliced the dawn. Accelerating to Mach 4, the missile raced through half of its four-mile journey in less than three seconds.

The F-16's radar beacon shut off as the weapon's seeker awoke. The AIM-120 AMRAAM missile's radar illuminated the *Colorado*'s sail. During the end of its flight, the AMRAAM computed the millisecond at which to detonate.

A wall of compressed air from the forty-eight-pound warhead smacked the vertical sail and dented it inward. A ring of slicing metal traced a cone through the *Colorado*'s right fairwater plane.

As waterlogged heaviness reclaimed the *Colorado*, Layne watched it submerge with the outer third of its sheared right fairwater plane tumbling along the hull. He cursed as his second AMRAAM overshot the sinking target and splashed into the water.

Jake bent backwards over the ship's control panel. The AMRAAM explosion rang in his head, and his back felt bruised. He pushed himself upright and listened for jet engines but heard no trace of aircraft overhead.

He forced a yawn to pop his ears and discerned a rumbling noise. The *Colorado* tilled the sea with its bow and ground to a stop.

"We're on the bottom," Jake said. "We're safe for the moment, but we've got to get out of here."

He looked to Tiger, who offered an unreadable grin. Jake found the husky man's apparent lack of fear disturbing, especially when he himself was terrified.

"We're rising!" McKenzie said.

Jake felt the *Colorado* settle at a two-degree down angle.

"We're light aft," he said. "Pump from forward to after trim tanks. I don't want our rudder exposed."

McKenzie flipped switches that directed water between internal tanks. The downward angle leveled at minus half a degree.

"You have depth control?" Jake asked.

"I think so," McKenzie said.

"Make your depth eighty-two feet," Jake said.

"We're dropping, but not too bad. I think I can level us off," McKenzie said.

"Nice job," Jake said. "I'm speeding us up to get out of here. We'll make fifteen knots until we get ten feet of water under us, then we'll punch it into high gear."

Jake walked behind the periscopes and sank into a Naugahyde captain's chair. Renard approached him.

"I know you're tired," Renard said, "but we should examine the speed to noise tradeoff."

"Do I need to remind you about geometry?" Jake asked. "Every knot of speed increases the area of uncertainty geometrically for whoever's looking for us. We need speed."

"You know this ship well, but I would be wary of the flow noise at fifteen knots given the damage to our sail. We do not know how bad the damage is or how it will affect our flow noise."

"Fifteen knots is optimal," Jake said.

"How so?"

"With the damage to the sail, I'm making a judgment call. You have a better idea?"

"No, I do not, but I need a cigarette. Do you have my Marlboros?"

Jake laughed.

"Yeah, I'll get them. And as long as I'm up, I'll fire up sonar to see who's in this ocean with us."

★

As Major Layne flew back to Tyndall, a P-3 Orion, a high endurance aircraft, dropped its first sonobuoy three miles behind the *Colorado*.

The P-3 had been rushed into the sky from Naval Air Station Jacksonville. Double checks were skipped, and the aircraft was loaded with a quarter of its nominal sonobuoy and fuel load. The haste proved wise as the P-3 reached the *Colorado* just after it submerged.

Below the Orion, a cylinder cut through the waves and bobbed back to the surface. A radio antenna sent a signal to the Orion telling its crew that the sonobuoy had awoken.

The tethered hydrophone absorbed sound. It heard the crackle of a shrimp bed, the drone of the Orion's propeller blades, and the ninety-five-point-three-hertz frequency tonal of the *Colorado's* reactor coolant pumps.

CHAPTER FIFTEEN

L ANCE RYDER SAT AMONG THE Secretaries of State and Defense, the National Security Advisor, the Joint Chiefs, and the Director of Central Intelligence in the White House's situation room. An outer circle of support personnel sat behind their leaders.

By six in the morning, security boats from Kings Bay had reached the *Colorado*'s survivors. Ryder understood that Lieutenant Jacob Slate was behind the '*Colorado* Incident'. Armed men of unknown origin had joined him, as had several missing *Colorado* crewmembers.

Ryder studied the Chief of Naval Operations, Admiral James Mesher, a gaunt, leather-faced submariner.

"Admiral," Ryder said, "the NORAD jets didn't keep the *Colorado* from submerging sooner than the hour you told me it needed."

"No, Mister President. The hijackers submerged in very shallow water. Based on the way they resurfaced before slipping under again, they probably hit bottom."

"So maybe they took some damage?"

"Yes, sir, possible damage with that impact and damage from the NORAD assets. They'll be loud, and I'm confident we can track them down."

"I think that statement is a little cavalier, especially given that I'm the first president to lose control of functional nuclear weapons."

Mesher opened his mouth but Ryder hushed him with a raised finger. He treated his Joint Chiefs harshly to command their attention, and he wouldn't soften in this crisis.

"How many warheads, Admiral?"

"Twenty-four missiles of six warheads each equates to one hundred and forty-four warheads, Mister President."

"And how big is each warhead?"

"Twenty times bigger than the one dropped on Nagasaki."

"Marvelous. A naval vessel designed to be undetectable by even today's technology, carrying almost three thousand times the destructive force of the bomb dropped on Nagasaki, is in the hands of a twenty-six year old renegade American naval officer."

Ryder glanced around the table to ensure that he held everyone's interest. He turned back to the CNO.

"We've lost control of a Trident Missile submarine. We hardly chinked its armor, we're tracking it with a solitary aircraft that's running short on sonobuoys, and we're still three and a half hours away from being able to hit the damn thing with a legitimate weapon. Is this correct, Admiral?"

"Yes, sir," Mesher said.

"And can the *Colorado* launch its nuclear weapons?"

"No, sir," Mesher said. "That's impossible without access to launch codes assigned specifically to the *Colorado's* launch system."

"What other nuclear threat does this rogue submarine now pose?" Ryder asked.

"Sir, the most it can do is jettison dormant weapons. The missiles cannot fly and there is no way that a static detonation of a warhead can take place."

"But could someone defeat the safeguards?"

"Impossible, sir. The detonator circuits are buried within the warheads, which are inaccessible from inside the ship. Even if they could access the circuitry, the hijackers would have to trick the circuits into believing they were in high-speed flight and at altitude. To do that, they'd need top-secret schematics that I've verified have not been compromised."

Ryder glanced around the table.

"What other scenarios are we facing? What if this ship finds its way to a hostile party?"

Rick McAllistar, the Director of Central Intelligence, slid a report under Ryder's nose. Ryder took note that a crisis of global implication appeared to be business as usual to him.

"Mister President, this is a list of the top twenty organizations that could be behind this. You'll notice that five of the top ten, and nine of the top fifteen, are Middle Eastern nations or groups they support."

"I can't let the Middle East do this to us," Ryder said.

David Rankin, the National Security Advisor, faced Ryder. The man reminded him of a Wall Street broker, but Ryder appreciated that Rankin was fearless in voicing his opinion.

"Sir, we can turn this to our advantage. Preliminary reports state that the mercenaries exposed swarthy skin through their ski masks. If we leak this, America will draw its own conclusion. It will build support for our military effort in the Middle East."

"Christ! I was hoping to keep this from the media altogether," Ryder said.

"Sir, there are more than thirty firsthand witnesses and many more working the rescue operation," Rankin said.

"They're military personnel. They can be trusted to keep this sealed."

"The entire Kings Bay naval submarine base and their families will know about this before lunchtime, Mister President. Word will get out that a Trident submarine is missing. That can't be covered up."

"Damn it, I know that! I mean that we can spin the ship's absence to appear accidental and then put a gag on the few who know the truth."

"Like a reactor accident?" Rankin asked.

"Exactly. We can say that a reactor malfunction drove a volunteer crew to take the ship to sea. Then after we sink the ship we can say it was scuttled to ensure reactor containment. That might work, am I right, Admiral?"

"If we contain the witnesses," Mesher said. "The *Colorado's* duty crew and rescue personnel are being assembled in a waterfront briefing room and will remain isolated under guard. But there were several injured personnel transported to the Naval Air Station, Jacksonville Hospital."

"That hospital is a military installation. Order the men isolated and guarded," Ryder said.

Ryder placed his fingers to his lips and contemplated aloud.

"Even after we sink this ship," he said, "it's going to haunt us."

"That could be the point, sir," McAllistar, the DCI said. "Perhaps this was a move to weaken our image, or to strengthen the image of a particular leader within the Middle East. We risk embarrassment if we sink it."

"We have only two choices," Rankin said. "Sink it or not. The only risk in sinking it is that we lose an aging submarine and face a radioactive cleanup operation. The choice is clear."

"I agree," Ryder said. "Admiral Mesher, sink the *Colorado*."

Ryder took a deep breath. He had made the decision he had to make. Next, he turned his attention to diplomacy and his Secretary of State.

"What did you dig up, Sandra?" he asked.

"I've contacted representatives of the major governments who are suspected of supporting Middle East extremist organizations," she said. "If they know about the *Colorado* Incident, they're keeping poker faces."

"I assume you didn't tip our hand?"

"Don't worry, Mister President. I told each man separately that you wanted to meet with him today, using no-fly zones as a dummy topic. My conversations were short, but none of them reacted as if they were hiding anything. I can usually tell."

"That doesn't rule out the possibility that a faction within the Middle East is involved without the major nations knowing about it," Rankin said. "The sooner we let America know that this is an act of Middle Eastern aggression, the sooner we'll have support for the escalated military action we need."

"We've got to be cautious," Ryder said. "I see no need to reveal anything until we sink the *Colorado* and put this behind us."

Ryder heard a pen scribbling notes behind him. He turned and examined Derrick Banks, his personal aide. Banks wore a short, auburn goatee that complimented his brown freckles.

"I think we should reconsider sinking the *Colorado*."

A murmur enveloped the room. Ryder raised a finger.

"Quiet!" he said. "We have an hour and a half until we sink it. Go on, Derrick."

"The most important facet of this incident is the *Colorado*'s ultimate destination," Banks said. "If we sink the ship, we'll never know who took it."

"In an operation like this," Rankin said, "there'll be a trail of evidence."

"We don't know what type of operation this is," Banks said. "If this were an act of war or terrorism, how do you explain their sparing the entire duty crew and not attacking the nearest major U.S. city? They could have torpedoed Jacksonville's harbor or melted down their reactor to contaminate hundreds of thousands of people before we even knew the *Colorado* was missing."

"So what are they doing?" Ryder asked.

"My guess is that someone took the *Colorado* to get to its warheads," Banks said.

"Why?" Ryder asked. "They can't be detonated."

"A group with technical backing could salvage and reuse the warheads – or the warheads could be easily converted into radioactive dirty bombs to spread contamination."

"Good point," Ryder said. "But why should this change our decision to sink the ship?"

"The hijackers are using the *Colorado* as a transport vehicle. Assuming we're dealing with highly trained extremists, we won't take the hijackers alive. Their bodies will be untraceable, and all trails of evidence will run into dead ends. If we don't follow the *Colorado*, we'll never know who took it."

Ryder never changed his mind easily. He pondered Banks' words.

"Admiral Mesher," he said, "how feasible is the idea of following the Trident to its destination?"

The old admiral's green eyes sparkled as Ryder gave him the opportunity to recover what he'd lost.

"The best way to keep tabs on one submarine is by placing another submarine behind it," Mesher said. "I can place a submarine behind the *Colorado* in five hours."

"Or we can sink the *Colorado* with a torpedo from an aircraft before this gets out of hand," Rankin said. "The best option is to destroy it immediately."

Ryder studied the pursed lips and furrowed brows of his non-naval military chiefs. Their silent agreement with Rankin's plan was obvious, but he wasn't swayed.

"We can always sink the *Colorado*, but we can't 'un-sink' it," Ryder said. "Keep the weapon-bearing assets in pursuit of the *Colorado*, but while we're waiting for them to get there, let's also work on a plan to follow it."

CHAPTER SIXTEEN

A TEMPEST SWIRLED IN JOHN Brody's mind. An encrypted order had just dashed his hopes of returning home to reconstruct his marriage. Instead, he had to whip the *Miami* into shape to race battle-ready toward an unknown point in the ocean. His squadron commodore had awakened him with a phone call to confirm that the order came from Admiral Mesher himself.

"Okay, Admiral Mesher. Let's see what you've got me doing out here," Brody said.

From his personal safe, he pulled a codebook that contained a simple one-for-one character exchange that varied daily. He thumbed through to 'May 11th' and placed his message through a second decryption.

The first lines of text revealed that the message was an operational order from the Chief of Naval Operations. The content told him he was tasked to hunt his best friend, Jake Slate.

He climbed the stairs to the control room. His weapons officer stood as Officer of the Deck.

"Captain, the ship is rigged for dive, crossing the dive point. The control party has reviewed the shallow water diving procedure."

Brody gave permission to submerge. The *Miami* spewed white foam from its ballast tanks and slipped into the ocean. An experienced crew shifted water about the boat and settled the *Miami* with methodic control under the surface of the Atlantic.

"Officer of the Deck, shift the reactor to high-speed pumps. Increase ship's speed to flank. Come to course one-four-zero," Brody said.

The weapons officer looked back at him through Coke-bottle glasses.

"Sir, it's my duty to remind you that our speed and depth combination are in violation of this vessel's submerged operations safety parameters."

"Weapons officer, have the Quartermaster annotate in the deck log that I'm authorizing violation of the submerged operations envelope. After that, announce that there is a meeting in the wardroom for all officers. When you hear what this mission is really about, you'll understand."

★

Jake's memory of the attacking jets had blurred. He remembered being scared and feeling lucky to be alive. Stuck in a ship with a squad of commandos and a mysterious Frenchman, he felt alone. He distracted himself with tactics and thought about the jagged metallic edges on his damaged sail creating babbling broadband flow noise. He grabbed a microphone.

"Maneuvering, control room, make turns for eight knots."

"Jake," Renard said, "I bit my tongue as you drove us into the sea floor. You must make calls in a crisis, and I'm betting my life that you're capable. But I prefer that you confer with me on tactical decisions."

"You're the one who wanted to slow last time we talked about it."

"That was hours ago," Renard said.

"Look, Renard," Jake said, "it's my ship and my call."

"But I'm an authority figure for the Taiwanese. We cannot afford to have them see you and me divided. I should be involved with decisions. And please, in private, call me Pierre."

"Okay, Pierre. I'll confer with you when I can, but at the end of the day it's my ship, and I make the decisions."

"But you must agree that when you're sleeping and I'm on watch, you will have to deal with my decisions. And I mean more than just with tactics. I have influence with the Taiwanese aboard this vessel. You must appreciate that."

"You may know these commando killers, but even you can't keep the reactor running long term," Jake said. "Only I understand this pig completely. If you or any of these commando goons mess with me, you'll find yourselves floating in a coffin you don't understand."

To his chagrin, Jake realized just how much his French companion enjoyed arguing.

"I agree that you have knowledge of this ship that I will never have, but I'm capable of learning the reactor plant. I've learned several before. It might take me time to understand its basic operations, but I can do it."

"Enough to go under the ice?" Jake asked.

"No, but I could deviate from our plan and go the long way around South Africa. I merely wish to point out that your power over me is not absolute."

Renard inhaled from his Marlboro.

"I only recruit people whom I can respect and trust," Renard said. "I wish that you could trust me. By ignoring my counsel and suspecting my every move, you place this entire ship at risk."

★

While Mike Gant roamed the engine room and shifted machinery to slower, quieter modes of operation, Jake entered maneuvering and addressed David Bass.

"I know you could do this yourself, but I thought I'd give you some moral support. You've been kicking butt back here, by the way," Jake said.

"Thanks," Bass said. "Are we crazy?"

"We're crazy to the tune of millions. Just do what I tell you and we'll get through this. Shift the reactor to natural circulation."

Bass' belly jiggled as he pulled handles upward. Pumps shut off within the reactor, extinguishing the *Colorado*'s power-driven reactor coolant flow. Pressurized water in the core heated up, rose via convection to steam generators, released energy, and fell back into the core.

The natural, heat-driven convection drove cooling water through the core with a whisper.

"I'm going back up front," Jake said. "You'll have to keep things cool back here. Remember to watch the xenon build up. I don't want this plant shutting itself down."

★

The P-3 Orion that had been scrambled from Jacksonville ascertained the *Colorado*'s course of one-four-zero, to the southeast, moving between seven and nine knots. It dropped its last sonobuoy and turned for shore as its fuel gauge dipped into its reserves.

A P-3 Orion from Puerto Rico fully loaded with fuel, sonobuoys, and torpedoes reached the *Colorado*. The P-3's hot-swapped data, and track on the Trident stayed solid during the exchange. At sunrise, a sonar technician became alarmed as he sipped from his cup of coffee. The crisp, baritone whine of the *Colorado*'s reactor coolant pumps had disappeared.

★

President Ryder heard the CNO's gritty voice.

"The *Colorado* has slowed and secured her reactor coolant pumps," Mesher said. "Our P-3 Orion has lost contact but is trying to regain it."

"How does this affect our ability to track the *Colorado*?" Ryder asked

"The silent operations confirm that the hijackers don't want us to find them, but the reduced speed works to our advantage in letting the *Miami* reach the *Colorado* sooner."

"What if we can't regain control?" Ryder asked.

The Air Force Chief of Staff lashed out.

"We need to sink that ship! This is already an unacceptable risk. That submarine could be minutes away from launching missiles."

"Impossible!" Mesher said. "A team of experts couldn't bypass the safeguards, and the *Miami* is on station and will take control of the situation. We were caught off guard but have responded flawlessly. I'm sending capable people to deal with this. Let them do their jobs."

CHAPTER SEVENTEEN

SHOWERED AND WEARING HIS BLUE jumpsuit, Jake stood by the port side periscope. He glanced at Renard, who sat in a dark corner of the control room at the electronic sensory measures suite.

"ESM is ready," Renard said.

"Very well. Raising number two scope," Jake said.

Jake sought a GPS fix of his location, but as he glued his eye to the rising steel cylinder, an alarm whined, and he lowered the scope.

"What is it?" Jake asked.

"*Merde*! An APS-137 radar at high signal strength. That's a P-3 Orion submarine killer overhead."

"Do you recommend altering course?" Jake asked.

He knew the answer but found comfort conferring with the ex-commander of the *Amethyst*.

"Yes, now may be a good time to head for the shipping lanes. Don't change speed. Any faster, and the P-3 might hear us."

★

In the *Miami*'s wardroom, Brody explained the mission.

"The CNO himself is behind this one," he said. "It's happening, it's real, and it's us."

"Sir, do we have intelligence on the expected resistance from the *Colorado*?" Pete Parks, his executive officer, asked in a Texas drawl. "Can we assume it has torpedoes ready?"

"Weapons ready, yes. A crew to support a long-term engagement, no. But we're not going to shoot unless provoked. This is an intelligence gathering mission. We won't destroy the *Colorado* until we learn where it's going and who's waiting for it. It'll be my judgment when we've reached that point."

A knock on the wardroom door interrupted him. A young sailor entered.

"Sir, the Officer of the Deck reports that the ship has received bell ringer sonar contact from a P-3 and requests permission to ascend to periscope depth."

Brody took the *Miami* shallow, received data on the *Colorado*'s new course, then returned deep. Slowing the *Miami* to listen for the Trident, he heard the gritty voice of Senior Chief Schmidt, his senior sonar technician, bellow over a loudspeaker.

"Control room, sonar room, we have a submerged contact, bearing zero-three-six. Trident Missile submarine! Designate sierra thirty-seven. We've got its distillate brine pump."

Schmidt was the best Brody had seen. He had met him on the *Florida* and had made sure that Schmidt joined him when he took command of the *Miami*.

"Attention in the control room," Brody said. "Make all torpedo tubes ready, enter firing solutions for sierra thirty-seven, the USS *Colorado*. Make tube one the primary firing weapon. Make tube two the backup.

"Weapons officer," Brody said, "I don't want to slow down to come to periscope depth now. Get a SLOT buoy ready stating we're holding contact on the *Colorado* and launch it from the three-inch launcher."

Minutes later, a submarine launched, one-way transmission buoy ascended from the *Miami*. As it reached the ocean's surface, the SLOT buoy's antenna jutted upward and linked to an orbiting satellite. The satellite recognized the top priority signature from the USS *Miami* and relayed the data.

★

Jake inched the *Colorado* toward the Gibraltar trans-Atlantic shipping lanes. Cautious, he again took the *Colorado* to periscope depth but found no radar systems. A GPS fix showed that the gyroscopic navigators were accurately tracking the ship's position. Assuming his plan back on track, Jake joined the Frenchman by one of the fire control screens.

"McKenzie energized the basic sonar system," he said. "So let's get on with your lesson. See this screen?"

"It shows time versus direction?"

"Time-bearing plot."

"Useful for surface ships and other loud contacts. Poor against quiet submarines. Can I solve course and speed automatically on this screen?" Renard asked.

"Yes. The system is automatic, but I'm going to hold you responsible for backing up the machine with your own mental target motion analysis."

"I remember target motion analysis. These machines and the principles behind them are familiar enough that I do not need to be coddled through your lessons."

"Okay, Einstein, I'll go faster."

"I'm merely trying to make good use of your time. You look fatigued. Maybe I could run things from the control room while you get some sleep. I've been awake all day, yet you've been up longer," Renard said.

Jake felt drained.

"Okay," he said. "I'm going down. Wake me if you solve for a contact within eight miles or if they need help in the engine room."

★

President Ryder returned from a White House lunch with a visiting dignitary. He hoped the public appearance would curtail speculation as the *Colorado* Incident hit the national news.

Journalists caught him on camera returning from the affair, but none were permitted close enough to ask questions. Ryder swallowed bile, smiled, and waved at the cameras. He felt the discomfort of indigestion as he returned to the situation room.

President Ryder noticed that the lines of stress on Admiral Mesher's face were diminishing.

"Mister President," Mesher said, "the USS *Miami* is in a trail position on the *Colorado*. The lead P-3 Orion is breaking contact. We have another P-3 on station, and two more submarines will be there in eight hours to set a battle-space perimeter around the *Colorado* and *Miami*."

"Finally, some good news," Ryder said.

"We have some insight into what might have motivated Lieutenant Slate," Rankin, the NSA said. "According to one of his colleagues, he claims to have been infected with HIV from Commander Henry, the *Colorado*'s commanding officer. He also claims there was a cover up."

"How did this happen? Is this confirmed?"

"It was an accident at sea followed by Henry donating blood to Slate. The accident is confirmed. The HIV issue and a supposed cover up are dubious. We questioned Henry. He's shaken by the circumstances, and when we mentioned Slate's HIV accusation he refused to talk."

"Damn!" Ryder said. "There might be something to this."

"Henry is locked down tight with the rest of the crew, so he's not going anywhere. It appears that Slate thought he had a score to settle."

"A mission of vengeance?" Ryder asked.

"Perhaps, sir, but it's doubtful he's doing this without help. The commandos involved in this behaved like well trained professionals. They are likely sponsored, and Slate's personal financial history didn't show that he moved enough money to fund mercenaries."

"Then this news of Slate's HIV doesn't get us any closer to knowing who's supporting him," Ryder said.

"It suggests his motivation," Rankin said.

"But we still need to trail the submarine to put the pieces together."

"I challenge that, Mister President," Rankin said. "We can project the *Colorado*'s destination. The ship's course places it en route to Gibraltar. Cross-referencing the DCI's list leads to Libya and Algeria.

We have this narrowed down enough to finger our culprits through other means."

"There's something wrong with your Mediterranean theory," Mesher said. "Transit through the Straits of Gibraltar doesn't make sense. Four countries operate underwater fixed hydrophone arrays at the Straits. Combine this with a multitude of anti-submarine warfare assets operating in the region, and the Straits of Gibraltar is an impenetrable choke point."

"The admiral's making sense," Ryder said. "It's too soon to implicate the Mediterranean states. I'm not ready to deviate from our plan."

"The heat from the media will only grow," Rankin said. "It's already been leaked to the national news. You'll need to address this publicly soon."

"My White House spokesman can buy us time."

"He can handle initial press conferences, Mister President, but he can only say nothing for a limited time, maybe two days," Rankin said. "But you'll need to stand at the podium in no later than seventy-two hours."

"If we do our jobs and get lucky," Ryder said, "this will be over by then."

★

Almost two days had elapsed since the *Colorado* had left port. Sounds from transiting cargo ships and freighters filled its bow-mounted spherical sonar as the Trident crawled at eight knots below the Gibraltar transit lanes.

The *Colorado*'s eleven-man skeleton crew had split into sections of five and six, the second having Jaguar as a spare body. One section ran the ship from noon to midnight, and then the other took over.

Jake led one section's affairs in the control room with Cheetah handling the rudder and planes. At the ship's control panel, Kao memorized the location of buttons and switches but relied upon Jake's instructions for operations. The rest of the section consisted of Gant controlling the engine room in maneuvering and Leopard patrolling the plant's vast spaces.

Renard ran the other section using Scott McKenzie to handle the ship's control panel and answer questions about shipboard systems. David Bass ran the engine room, paired with Panther.

There was little time for sleep during the twelve hours off duty as the men brought the ship's systems online. With torpedoes electronically mated to the fire control system, the hijackers had firepower. After deploying a towed array sonar hydrophone system, they could hear all around them from a line of hydrophones streaming behind the *Colorado*.

★

Renard stared at a screen full of sonar data. Jake sat beside him.

"So, your rest served you well?" Renard asked.

"I was wiped out," Jake said.

"I look forward to my turn to sleep."

"Soon," Jake said. "First I want to show you our towed array sonar display. Mister Lion and I just rolled the hydrophones out. Are you familiar with it?"

Renard followed Jake's finger to the display of squiggly lines he thought he remembered how to decipher.

"If I interpret this correctly, that's the array's nose, the direction in which we're pulling it. The middle of the display represents the beam, or the perpendicular bisection of the array, correct?"

"That's right," Jake said. "You see these three fuzzy lines trickling down the screen? Do they correlate with what you've been tracking on the spherical sonar?"

Standing, Renard felt light headed and numb. He needed sleep.

"Yes, precisely. I have three merchant vessels on the sphere," Renard said, "and I'm tracking them in the fire control system. I entered the sonar room and listened to verify that they sounded like merchants. There are no warships in our vicinity."

"Yeah, the merchant traces look fuzzy like they're made by poorly machined screws," Jake said. "It looks like we're undetected. I relieve you. Get some sleep."

Renard crept down the staircase. As befitting his role on the *Colorado*, he entered the executive officer's quarters. Lying in his rack, he assessed Jake Slate.

Although possibly lucky, the American had shown good judgment. He had risked bottoming the ship to submerge as soon as possible, and that decision had minimized damage by the jet fighter attack. Also, Renard thought that by slowing to eight knots, Jake might have already saved the *Colorado* from a P-3 Orion attack.

He complimented himself for identifying Jake's potential but reflected upon the mission off the Russian coast and wondered if deceit could victimize him twice. He made a note in his tired mind to remain wary of Jake. He also pondered the threats outside of the *Colorado*'s hull. Countless submarines, surface combatants, and aircraft surely hunted them, but for the moment, he comforted himself with the thought that the *Colorado* appeared to be alone.

As sleep overcame him, he thought of the only person whom he knew still meant anything to him, Marie Broyer. She filled his dreams.

In his dream, a strong gust carried the sweet scent of lilac across Renard's face. His hands felt warm stone as he sat on a slab of sun-bathed granite.

Examining the view below a clear sky, he recognized a summit he had climbed often during his boyhood in France's Provincial region. Atop Mont Saint Victoire, the peak gracing Paul Cezanne's impressionist paintings, Renard looked around.

To his left, fertile valleys of green and sunflowers. To his right, the rocky mountaintop. Below him, the dirt and underbrush that blanketed the eastern slope. Renard felt peace in this image of his past.

He spied a figure seated next to him out of the corner of his eye. He recognized a loving voice.

"Pierre?"

"Marie?" he asked, but the figure was gone.

Storm clouds invaded the dream and turned the sky dark. A gust felt cold on his face as a second voice startled him.

"Pierre!"

Standing over him, blocking the scant sunlight that pushed through approaching storm clouds, loomed the figure of an American naval officer wearing a deep blue cotton jump suit. Flame had charred the embroidered nametag that displayed Jake Slate's name. A blood-caked tear at the shoulder appeared to have been carved by animal claws.

The Jake-image pointed a pistol up the mountain. Renard looked to the summit, but the peak had disappeared into black clouds. Covered in sweat and grime, Jake's face looked agonized. His eyes were filled with rage.

"Pierre, come with me. I need you!"

"Me? Why? I thought you did not trust me."

"Come with me. I need you!" Jake said.

"Why? Where are we going?"

"You know where we're going."

Lightning crashed. Jake tucked his pistol in his belt and started up the mountain.

"We're going to die," Jake said.

Lightning cracked again, and Renard awoke.

CHAPTER EIGHTEEN

"WHAT DO YOU HAVE, EXECUTIVE officer?" Brody asked from the captain's chair in the *Miami's* control room.

"Sir, we presently hold sierra thirty-seven, the USS *Colorado*, at twelve thousand, five hundred yards, just over six miles," Parks said. "Course and speed haven't changed."

"Got it. Thanks for covering things last night. I needed the rest."

Brody had hardly slept while hunting Jake. He questioned if his friend had gone insane, but with the bitterness of his failing career, he also wondered if the Navy might have done something to set him off. Frustrated that he might deliver judgment without knowing the truth, Brody had only been able to sleep after giving in to exhaustion.

"Sir," Parks said. "Some of the guys say you know Slate pretty well."

"I do. Or at least I thought I did."

"He's your friend?"

"Yeah?"

"You want to talk about it?" Parks asked.

Brody felt Parks studying him. Despite the temptation of oblivion gnawing at him, he had kept the bottle at bay while underway, but he sensed Parks' suspicion.

"You've got something on your mind, Pete?"

"You're under enough stress already, sir. I can't imagine what it's like having a friend of yours go nuts and all. Then being tasked to kill him."

"We don't have to kill him," Brody said.

"Come on, sir. The brass back home wants a flowery ending where we figure out who's behind this theft and recapture the *Colorado* in one piece, but you and I both know there aren't a heck of a lot of scenarios where everyone gets out of this alive."

Brody feared Parks was right but clung to the optimism that he needed to stay in balance. He wouldn't let Parks upset that.

"It's entirely possible, Pete. And don't you for a second abandon the idea that it isn't."

"Well, sir," Parks said, "it's just that–"

"You think I've gone soft because I know Slate?"

"Just volunteering the possibility, sir."

"You just do your job," Brody said. "And unless I ask, don't bring it up again."

For the first time while Parks was his executive officer, Brody thought he saw defiance in his face. The vision unsettled him.

"Okay sir," Parks said. "I have a recommendation."

"Go ahead."

"I think we should open range."

"Why?"

"To avoid counter-detection."

"Our orders are to keep our thumb on Slate," Brody said. "If we drift too far behind and can't hear him, then we could miss something. I don't want to risk that."

"The sound propagation environment supports hearing him out another three thousand yards."

"He's got a skeleton crew and can't hold a constant alert state. He's not looking hard over his shoulder."

"I think we don't lose anything by backing off, though, sir."

Brody wasn't sure if he refuted Parks' advice for tactical reasons or to keep his executive officer in check.

"No. We're staying right where we are."

★

Jake noticed that the Frenchman's eyes were puffy from sleep.

"Have you considered doing a baffle clear to see if someone is trailing us?" Renard asked.

"It's too noisy. But we could deploy the thin line towed array."

"You have another towed array sonar?"

"We hardly use it," Jake said.

"Is it inferior to the towed array sonar we have deployed now?"

"It's better, actually, except you've got to slow below five knots to make good use of it, and if you go above fifteen knots it gets sucked into the screw. Design flaw."

"It's worth deploying this and slowing, do you not think? We're not in a hurry. Our rendezvous is still a day away."

Jake summoned McKenzie to deploy the thin line array. Thirty minutes later, McKenzie returned from the engine room with the task complete.

"Are we ready then?" Renard asked.

"Let's go to the sonar room," Jake said. "We have to view the thin line readout on a special monitor."

Jake flipped a switch and a screen came to life. He noticed a new, faint trace toward the back portion of the acoustic field of view.

"We've got a problem," he said. "Looks like a sixty-hertz tonal in our baffles."

"All American vessels run sixty-hertz electric plants. It could be a distant merchant," Renard said.

"In our baffles, with no other tonal noise?"

"I was trying to be optimistic."

"We've got company. Stay close to me and speak up if you think I'm doing something stupid," Jake said.

Jake called his skeleton crew to the control room. He read concern in their faces.

"We may have a submarine behind us," Jake said. "Scott, take Mister Jaguar and load countermeasures into the three-inch launchers.

Gant, join Bass and get the plant ready for an emergency pump start to all ahead flank.

"Mister Cheetah and Mister Tiger, take seats at the control stations," Jake said. "Shift stern plane control to Mister Tiger. Keep the rudder and fairwaters with Mister Cheetah. Mister Lion, stay here. I want you on the circuit with maneuvering."

Jake turned the ship and returned to the thin line display in the sonar room where he conferred again with Renard.

"See that trace in our tail area?" he asked. "Now that we've turned, I'm looking for it to move. It'll shift relative to our ship's direction, but I'm looking for its geographical bearing to stay the same. But if it moves and passes back into our baffles, we have a problem."

Ten minutes later, the *Colorado* had settled on a new course, and Jake pointed to the thin line screen.

"The sound trace is moving back into our baffles," he said. "It's close, whatever it is."

"*Merde!* We're being trailed."

"Let's try one more thing. Let's steady on our original course and see what the trace does then."

"Exactly what I would have done with the *Amethyst*," Renard said.

Ten minutes passed as Jake watched the trace settle in the baffles again.

"We've got to break trail," he said. "We'll slowly speed up and try to open distance – get a little breathing room while our trailer doesn't notice. Then we'll hit the all ahead flank bell, launch countermeasures, and change course."

"I agree. Our trailer may already suspect that we've counter-detected him."

"I need you to handle this," Jake said.

"You would entrust this to me?"

"I have to. I need to supervise the reactor plant. Starting coolant pumps is a rapid introduction of cold water. That's going to excite the core, and if we screw up, the reactor trips offline."

"I've developed an adequate sense for the way this vessel handles under normal conditions, but nothing near the limits of its performance."

"Do you remember the acceleration times and turning rate of the *Amethyst*?"

"I will never forget them."

Jake yelled as he slid down the ladder.

"Whatever they are," he said, "double them for this pig!"

Jake passed through the circular hatch to the engine room, reached maneuvering, and greeted Bass. He then called Renard and told him he was ready. Seconds later he heard the Frenchman's voice over the loudspeaker.

"Breaking trail!" Renard said. "All ahead flank. Scott, launch the three inch launcher."

Jake faced the reactor panel. David Bass stood one panel over at the steam flow controls.

"Partial scramming rods," Jake said and twisted a partial scram switch. A pneumatic drive system thrust neutron-absorbing control rods into the core. Power gauges dipped low.

"Starting pumps. Answer ahead flank!" he said.

Jake shifted the *Colorado*'s reactor coolant pumps to top speed as Bass twirled a throttle wheel. The hiss of steam ringing through pipes filled the engine room, and the deck plates rumbled.

The phone rang, and Jake picked it up.

"Maneuvering," he said.

"Jake," Renard said. "We should launch a weapon."

"What? And piss off whoever's chasing us?"

"No, distract them. Make them worry about an incoming weapon so that they lose sight of us."

"I don't want to kill an innocent submarine."

"It would be unlikely," Renard said. "We would need abnormal luck."

Jake felt events happening too fast to analyze them to his satisfaction. Under duress, he found merit in the Frenchman's argument and followed his advice.

"Launch the weapon," he said.

★

Butterflies fluttered throughout President Lance Ryder's stomach as his aide handed him his speech.

"Mister President, the NSA told the press yesterday that they are not going to get detailed answers from you today. They want the truth, but they'll settle for a show of confidence. Your demeanor will tell them everything. You will buy the time you need to see this to its end."

"Thank you, Derrick," Ryder said.

"Remember, sir. This speech is short but important. Milk it."

Ryder walked from behind a curtain into the briefing room. Never before had the lights seemed so burning, the camera flashes so caustic.

"My fellow Americans, for three days the media has been telling you that a Trident submarine, a very powerful weapon, is missing."

His tone remained strong, his poise intact.

"The *Colorado* is presently engaged in an operation with details I cannot yet divulge for reasons of national security. I cannot tell you where the *Colorado* is or why it is there, but I will address your very valid concerns.

"The *Colorado* poses no danger to America or its allies, nor does it threaten world peace. The nuclear warheads onboard the *Colorado* are not, nor will ever be outside the control of our nation's military.

"The secrecy surrounding the *Colorado* is necessary. I appreciate the concern shown by the nation, and now I ask that you exercise trust. Trust in me and trust in the men and women of your military. I thank you for your understanding and for your concern."

Ryder exited from the podium, brushing the shoulder of a spokesman who was moving to face the onslaught of questions. He rejoined Banks behind a curtain.

"You performed well, sir," Banks said.

"We'll see how the media spins this, Derrick."

"Well, sir, I need to tell you something. I wanted to wait until your speech was finished. Perhaps you should sit down."

"No, damn it. Just spit it out!"

"China has launched an exercise attack against Japan. No weapons were launched and no peacetime rules of engagement were violated, but there are enough Chinese naval vessels near Japanese waters to cause concern. We interpret this as a warning to adhere to our policy of not interfering with Chinese affairs in Taiwan."

"What's the status in Taiwan?"

"The Chinese aren't calling it blockade, but that's what it is. They're still letting most shipping through, but they've proven they can halt fuel tankers and combatants. They disabled a tanker yesterday. They're flexing their muscles, sir."

"We've got war in the Middle East, a rogue Trident on the run, and now we've got China tightening the rope around Taiwan. Do you have any good news?"

"No, sir. Just be thankful the *Colorado* Incident is under control."

★

Brody heard Schmidt's voice over a speaker.

"Possible target zig, USS *Colorado*. Contact is speeding up. We've got excessive flow noise – probably water over damaged fairwater planes. We've got a ton of power plant transients."

Brody acknowledged the report and felt his throat tighten. He stood to announce his reaction but Schmidt's voice rang out again.

"Countermeasures! Compressed gas. We're blinded in the *Colorado's* sector."

"Any sign of a weapon?" Brody asked.

"Negative, but we can't hear very – shit! High-speed screws. Torpedo in the water!" Schmidt said.

"Give me a bearing!"

Schmidt announced the bearing to the high-speed screws, and the torpedo alarm, triggered by hydrophones on the *Miami's* hull, chimed. Brody silenced the alarm and verified that it agreed with Schmidt's assessment.

"Torpedo evasion!" he said.

Brody turned the *Miami* and ordered it to its fastest, flank speed. The ship shook, and the control room fell silent until Schmidt cut through the tension.

"Weapon is drawing aft," Schmidt said. "We're clear."

"Secure from torpedo evasion. Get me a bearing to the *Colorado*," Brody said.

"Still blinded in their sector," Schmidt said.

"I'm going through."

Brody turned the *Miami* toward the *Colorado* and punched through the wall of noise created by its countermeasures to listen for the fleeing Trident.

Although the sprinting Trident rattled a cacophony of noises, Brody saw only fuzzy lines on his sonar display. The *Miami*'s sonar system was deafened by its own high speed. Brody slowed his submarine.

A trace to the north appeared on the sonar screen, but chasing after that noise at top speed would cost the *Miami*'s ability to listen to it. Brody could either listen to the *Colorado* or chase it. He could not do both.

He felt a sinking feeling in his stomach.

★

Brody sprinted after the Trident for hours. At the end of each sprint, he drifted and listened, but he never regained the *Colorado*.

He marched into his stateroom and slammed the door, leaned back in his chair, then grabbed a phone.

"This is the captain. Get me the executive officer," he said.

"Parks here, sir."

"Lieutenant Commander Parks, station yourself as the Command Duty Officer and assume my duties. With the exception of weapons release, you have full authority. Until I say otherwise, you're running the show."

CHAPTER NINETEEN

THE THIRTY THOUSAND TON CARGO vessel *Custom Venture* had set sail from Santos, Brazil, stopping in Port-au-Prince, Haiti, to exchange freight. Loaded with dry storage, the ship steamed along the transit lane to the Straits of Gibraltar en route to Marseille, France.

Steel cans filled all but three of the containers. Of the three, one was welded watertight and empty. Another was filled with sand and welded shut. The final vessel contained an anti-submarine depth charge.

Two *Custom Venture* crewmen, Taiwanese Army Captain Chu Hsin-min and Sergeant Ding Mou-shih, had infiltrated the *Custom Venture* under cover as longshoremen. Baggy coveralls concealing forty-five caliber pistols, lock picking tools, and a pair of high-powered binoculars, Chu and Ding climbed to the weather decks.

Leaning against the ship's railing, Chu inhaled the salt air and raised binoculars to his eyes. He studied stars flickering against an indigo backdrop, traded the binoculars with Ding, and pointed at the sky in a feigned lesson of astronomy.

However, the heavens held less of Chu's interest than the horizon where he expected to see a surfaced submarine.

★

Ryder entered the situation room and looked at a clock. It had been thirteen hours since the *Miami* had lost the *Colorado*.

"Admiral Mesher, what's the status?" he asked.

"We still have the *Colorado* contained, Mister President. The submarines *Boise* and *Philadelphia* are holding fifty-mile perimeters on the northern and southern boundaries, and two P-3 Orions have established the western and eastern ends. Each platform is sweeping inward, closing down the perimeter. The *Miami* is conducting a spiraling search from the *Colorado's* last known position."

"Are we going to regain the *Colorado*?" Ryder asked. "Don't candy coat this."

"Sir, when the *Colorado* evaded, it lost its stealth-quieting advantage at twelve knots due to damage imposed by the F-16's. That either restricts the *Colorado's* speed or makes it easier to find."

"Enough with this game," the Air Force Chief of Staff said. "We need to sink this Trident!"

"We still maintain-" Mesher said.

"No, Admiral," Ryder said. "You've had your chance. The *Colorado* knows we're looking for it, and it's proven its hostile intent. As soon as it's found, sink it."

★

"Did you figure out who it was?" Jake asked.

He felt anxious about having been trailed, and he wanted to know who hunted him.

"I believe so," Renard said. "I compared the frequencies we recorded during the encounter with your database. I was afraid our pursuer might have been a *Virginia* or a *Sea Wolf*, but it was only a third-flight *Los Angeles* class submarine."

"Which one?" Jake asked.

"I've narrowed it down to three. The frequencies from the port turbine generator and the starboard reactor coolant pump matched the sonic records of the *Topeka*, the *Miami*, and the *Asheville* - of those still in commission."

Jake flipped through the pages of a copy of *Jane's Fighting Ships*. His chest tightened.

"*Topeka* and *Asheville* are based in Hawaii," he said.

"Then we were trailed by the *Miami*."

"Oh shit," Jake said.

"What's wrong?"

"It's John Brody, the best skipper in the fleet. His ship was the one we passed on the way out of Kings Bay."

Renard raised a Marlboro to his mouth and blew smoke.

"The best skipper in the fleet?" Renard asked. "Then I hope that the world will soon take us for dead."

★

An hour later, Jake inched the *Colorado* forward at three knots. To fight the slow ascent, he ordered a seven-degree down angle. Tiger pushed the stern planes to a full dive and Cheetah strained his thin arms against the fairwater control wheel. His body tingling with the numbness of lost sleep, Jake stood by the ship's control panel.

"How are we doing, Scott?" he asked.

"Every tank's pumped dry," McKenzie said. "It took a while without the trim pump."

Jake sensed that, in protest against lack of maintenance, the *Colorado* was breaking down. Its trim pump's motor controller had burned out.

"Hovering tank's full, though. Right?" Jake asked.

"It's the only thing keeping us under."

"That's what I want. We can't risk pumping air into our ballast tanks. There's no quiet way to get air into them, and I don't want anyone to know we're here."

Ten minutes later, Jake took in residual sunlight through the periscope. A green running light twinkled on the *Custom Venture*'s silhouette. He ordered the Taiwanese commandos to release the stern and fairwater planes and McKenzie to drain the hovering tanks half way.

Swiveling the periscope optics downward, Jake watched bioluminescence and whitewash skim over the rising missile deck as the *Colorado* inched to the surface.

Straining his eyes against the setting sun of the mid-Atlantic, Captain Chu saw the rectangular silhouette of the *Colorado*'s sail. He entered the cargo ship's superstructure, climbed four decks, and watched Ding apply his tools to a locked door that read 'Officers Only'.

With Ding behind him, he ascended another flight of stairs and pushed open a door to the captain's quarters.

The captain reclined in his bed reading a copy of <u>Newsweek</u>.

"What's this about?" Captain Eduardo Martino asked in Portuguese.

Chu brandished his pistol. Martino lowered his magazine and placed his reading glasses on a table.

"I have no intent of arguing with armed men," Martino said. "What do you want from me?"

"Stop the ship and prepare your crew for crane and line handling work," Chu said.

Chu escorted Captain Martino to the bridge and took control of the four-man piloting team.

"Stop the ship," Chu said.

"This is a large ship," Martino said. "This will take time. Do you want me to sound a backing bell?"

"No, coast to a stop as if you had suffered an engineering casualty. If you receive radio contact from another vessel, that is what you will say has happened."

"I must tell you that there is a vessel six hours behind us in the transit lane."

"That poses no problem."

"Why am I slowing my ship?"

"Off your starboard beam you will see a surfaced submarine in the moonlight."

Martino raised binoculars to his eyes.

"A submarine? Whose?" Martino asked.

"You will know soon enough."

The first mate, Hector Verdugo, had been on the bridge when Chu arrived with the captain as his prisoner. Verdugo's brown eyes flashed.

"What makes you think we will obey you blindly? You are two men with pistols against an entire crew."

Sergeant Ding leveled his pistol at the first mate. Chu grabbed his arm and shouted for control. He then withdrew a list from inside his coverall pocket.

"Hector Verdugo," Chu said. "Your wife is Isabella and your sons of three and five years are Javier and Luis. You live with them at 37 Rancho Palos Verdes in Sao Paulo."

"You bastard!" Verdugo said.

"Captain Martino," Chu said, "I have similar data for most of the men on board. If you value the safety of your wife and four children, you will do as I tell you."

Martino nodded reluctantly.

"Stop the ship," Chu said. "Cycle your starboard running light every thirty seconds. Make a skiff ready and prepare for crane operation and rigging."

Two miles behind the *Custom Venture*, the *Colorado* slid through the ocean's surface and glided to a stop. Through the periscope, Jake spied the spotlight of the approaching skiff and barked at McKenzie.

"I'm going up to the bridge. Get some tools ready for topside cleats. And bring a rope."

Climbing through the sail, Jake felt the crisp sea breeze that blew through the bullet holes. Reaching the moonlit bridge, he examined the damage caused by the jet fighters.

A missile had dented the starboard side inward and cleaved the outer tip of the right fairwater plane. Reflecting moonlight, explosive residue caked the bent and severed plane.

McKenzie placed a rucksack of tools on Jake's shoulder and tied a rope to a welded handle. Jake heaved his leg over the bridge, descended ladder rungs down to the fairwater plane, and caught a rope McKenzie had tossed. Hand over hand, he scaled to the deck.

When his sneakers reached steel, he looked for the approaching skiff. The small boat's light caught his eye, and he waved his arms.

"Over here! Toward the bow!" Jake said.

Jake heard the whir of an outboard engine as the skiff circled, slowed, and backed down beside the *Colorado*.

"I have been instructed to offer assistance," the third mate said. "I have a mooring line, wireless telephones, and a bridge-to-bridge radio."

Jake heard Kao land with a clunk behind him. Kao helped him turn over a half submerged cleat and tie the skiff alongside the *Colorado*.

Jake hurled the coiled end of the rope dangling from the fairwater plane to the mate. Holding the rope, the mate braved the rope-assisted jump and climbed onto the rounded bow of the *Colorado*. Jake helped him to the deck, and the third mate offered a waterproof bag.

"No thanks," Jake said. "My associate goes first."

Kao grabbed the bag, rifled through it for a wireless phone, and disappeared behind the sail. When the commando returned, he handed Jake the phone.

"I have confirmed with my associates that the mission is proceeding per plan," Kao said. "There is a text message containing codes to ten accounts totaling forty million American dollars."

Jake felt revitalized.

CHAPTER TWENTY

FROM THE BRIDGE, RENARD WATCHED the skiff roll in the light seas as it dragged a meandering nylon line toward the *Custom Venture.* Jake startled him by speaking through a mouthpiece to Kao below.

"Mister Lion, right five degrees rudder," Jake said.

"Coming to starboard may be too shallow," Renard said. "If you overshoot the *Custom Venture*, it will take half an hour to circle back."

"I won't miss."

"I suppose you have it all figured out."

"Something wrong?" Jake asked.

As Renard grabbed his Marlboro, a crisp breeze blew amber cinders onto his olive parka.

"I've bitten my tongue more than once on this mission."

"Just stick to my plan," Jake said.

"Your plan failed to account for the *Miami*."

Jake grunted.

"I do not mean to criticize," Renard said. "I'm simply trying to begin a dialogue. What must a man do to earn your confidence?"

"You want to know?" Jake asked.

Renard felt Jake's finger poke his sternum.

"In high school, Grant Mercer hardly left my side for three months after my mother died so that I wouldn't kill myself. Riley Demorse and I traded duty responsibilities whenever one of us was too exhausted to stand watch. John Brody gave me a family. What the hell have you done?"

"I offered you liberation," Renard said.

"You're only doing it because I'm giving you a Trident full of warheads. These guys, they..."

"Yes? These guys?" Renard asked.

"They were real friends."

"Ah, yet you may never see your real friends again."

"So what's your point?"

Renard tossed his Marlboro over the side and raised a fresh one to his lips.

"Men like you - like us - desire control. That's why you've trusted so few men in your life, and then only in situations of dire need. But when you lose those friends, you feel a gap that's not so easily filled. Loneliness, I believe it is called."

"I still have Grant."

"Do you? Are you sure he will be there to pluck you from the sea on the other side of the world?"

"I have the guys on this ship."

"Do you consider them friends? I doubt it. I may now be your only true friend," Renard said. "At some time during this journey, you will need to decide that I've earned your trust."

"And if I don't?"

"Then I pray that fate has no intention of placing more strafing aircraft or *Miami*'s in our path. Tell me, this accident you suffered where you suspected foul play and mentioned a sort of impotence. You've hinted that your captain was at fault, and your angst was obvious, but we've never discussed the details."

"Why should I?"

"It could be therapeutic."

"I'm not impotent."

"I never thought so, because you seemed far more enraged than depressed," Renard said. "Yet you refused an attractive woman's advances and mentioned that you were sexually incapable. I've tried to remain reserved about it but must inquire."

Jake lifted a mouthpiece to his lips.

"Rudder amidships," he said.

The *Colorado* veered toward the *Custom Venture's* starboard quarter.

"Much better," Renard said. "I now see your angle."

"I have HIV," Jake said, "because that fucker Thomas Henry gave it to me."

"*Mon Dieu*! How?"

"I'm one of four guys on the crew who had AB positive blood. The other three donated a pint each, but Henry made damn sure his got in me first."

For the first time, Renard empathized with his recruit's rage.

"Why?"

"To protect his own ass," Jake said. "After my accident was reported in the Kings Bay base paper, praising everyone who helped save my life, a few gay sailors – still in the closet, of course, because the Navy makes them hide behind the 'don't ask don't tell' policy – figured out that I had Henry's blood in me. One of them warned me. Wrote me a nice long anonymous letter explaining everything."

"Henry was gay?" Renard asked.

"Married but bi-sexual and part of a sex ring that disbanded when a few of them discovered they were HIV-positive. Henry was due to have his HIV discovered at the next blood screening."

Renard sucked his Marlboro to the butt and sought its replacement.

"And it would have ended his career?" he asked.

"Yeah," Jake said. "HIV-positive sailors can't deploy on combatant vessels."

"And so neither could you, after he infected you."

"Right."

"But he did not do this out of pure malice?"

"No," Jake said. "He cut one of his fingers in some sort of bullshit accident I'm sure he faked while running down the passageway to be by my side. Then he just laid his hand on me. Supposedly, he was trying to demonstrate concern for my well-being while I lay there bleeding, but he made damned sure there were witnesses."

Renard realized the extent of the evil.

"And blood flowed both ways," he said, "casting doubt on who infected whom?"

"You got it," Jake said.

"Did you not bring this to your chain of command?"

"No, Pierre, those assholes brought it to me. Commander Henry has already been selected for promotion to captain, and he's been deep-selected to replace the submarine community's only black admiral. John Brody deserves it, but they selected Henry because he played politics and the race card better, I guess."

"Deplorable," Renard said, "yet I see how men who place politics above valor may have rallied to protect the man."

"The Commodore and base admiral told me to keep it quiet until Henry commanded his last patrol. Then he would have been done with sea duty before the next periodic blood draw, and he would waltz through shore commands on his way to admiral, HIV or not."

"And you?"

"I was supposed to transfer to the Trident Training Facility for instructor duty the morning the *Colorado* left for patrol. No one onboard knew about it but me, Henry, and our yeoman. Then from there, I was supposed to fester while my dream of commanding a submarine died."

Renard chuckled. Jake narrowed his eyes and stared.

"No," Renard said. "I'm not laughing at you. Do you not see, *mon ami*? This horrific, callous event strikes you, and you lament your lost dream of commanding a submarine. Yet here you are, with my help, of course, and the *Colorado* is yours."

Renard thought he noticed Jake holding back a smile.

"Just worry about your own problems," Jake said.

"What do you mean?"

"I heard you talking on the wireless."

"You understood?"

"Caught a few choice words."

"Such as?"

"Such as *'je t'aime'*. Even a first year French student recognizes that as 'I love you'. I had no idea you had emotional baggage."

"Until recently," Renard said, "neither did I."

★

As parallel steel arms lifted the skiff to the *Custom Venture's* deck, Jake ordered the *Colorado* to all stop, then watched the cargo vessel's forward capstan winch pull the nose of the *Colorado* alongside.

His gaze fell to the back of the Trident where McKenzie and commandos climbed topside through the missile compartment hatch. They carried wrench sets, crowbars, and coils of nylon line.

Jake looked through the *Custom Venture's* open cargo bay door. A group of longshoremen, a mix of Latinos and Europeans, stood in artificial light in front of a background of towering steel crates.

"How should I address our man on the bridge?" he asked while fingering the controls to a bridge-to-bridge radio.

"Call him 'Captain'," Renard said.

"Captain, do you copy?" Jake asked.

"Yes, sir," a man with a Mandarin accent said.

"Do you have communications with the cargo bay?" Jake asked.

"Yes, sir."

"Stand by to receive our second mooring line."

"Mister Panther," Jake said into his sound-powered phone, "have Scott cast over the line."

From the *Colorado's* deck, Scott McKenzie tossed a rubber ball up to the *Custom Venture's* bay. The ball carried a string behind it, which in turn held the end of a nylon mooring line.

A *Custom Venture* worker fielded the ball and dragged at the string and rope until he held enough mooring line to wrap around a second capstan within the cargo ship.

The capstan wound the rope and pulled the *Colorado* flush against the *Custom Venture*. Men lowered rubber come-alongs to the water line to buffer the bumping ships.

McKenzie supervised commandos in removing buoy hatch covers. Two cranes from the cargo ship swung overhead. After the commandos snapped the steel hooks to the exposed buoys, McKenzie signaled Jake with a thumbs up.

"Release the buoys," Jake said.

A thump reverberated throughout the *Colorado* as a blast of compressed gas severed the links holding each buoy to its nest. Gas venting around them, the buoys jumped and were caught by the *Custom Venture*'s cranes.

McKenzie inspected the nests to verify that the hoisting paths were clear. He motioned with a counter-clockwise waving of his arm.

"Lift the buoys," Jake said.

Cranes hoisted buoys that resembled plastic orange garbage cans up the side of the *Custom Venture*.

"Buoys away. The rest is ready?" Jake asked.

"Yes, sir," Captain Chu said. "Chains have been connected between the three steel crates. I verified the detonator. My partner will set it."

"Very well. I have one order of business left. Send two inflatable life rafts down to my deck. After that's done, tell the ship's crew to slack the mooring lines so I can cast off. I've been surfaced too long already."

Over the *Colorado*, a bright yellow barrel - a pneumatically inflatable raft - dangled in a webbed cargo net. As the raft touched down, Jake watched McKenzie help two commandos hold it steady. The crane released the webbing and rose to retrieve another raft.

McKenzie and the commandos rolled the rafts into the vacant buoy holes, bolted the buoy hatches over them, and prepared the *Colorado*'s topside to submerge again.

"Captain, make sure you follow my plan," Jake said as he watched McKenzie shut the hatch and seal the *Colorado*.

"Detonation will occur twelve hours from now," Chu said. "I will see to it."

"I hope so. If not, you might want to stay on the higher decks. Because if I don't hear crates hitting the water within the hour, I will be pumping this ship full of torpedoes. Now get this ship out of my way, and make sure its rudder is over hard right so you don't scrape my hull."

Jake led Renard down through the sail as the *Custom Venture* slipped away from the *Colorado*. He stared at the ship's control panel and McKenzie's grime-covered face. Cheetah and Tiger were seated at the control yokes, and the rest of the commandos had assembled to observe.

"The bridge is sealed, Scott. Fill all tanks."

Two hours after surfacing, the Trident slipped beneath the water.

★

Illuminated by floodlights, a crane swung a three-crate network containing the *Colorado's* identification buoys across the *Custom Venture's* deck. The crane lowered the network into the ocean, releasing it to Jake's calculations and the laws of physics.

Captain Chu watched the first crate, filled with sand, slide under the ocean surface. Dragged by the first, the empty second crate followed. The final crate, empty sans the *Colorado's* buoys and a depth charge strapped to its wall, kept the network afloat.

"The depth charge is pressure activated, sir," Chu said. "It will not detonate on the surface."

"You leave me no choice but to share your optimism," Captain Martino said.

"Our work here is complete," Chu said. "You may now continue your voyage to Marseille. My partner and I will be your personal escorts for the remainder of the voyage."

CHAPTER TWENTY-ONE

WEARING A TRENCH COAT OVER a charcoal Brooks Brothers sport coat and a black turtleneck, Grant Mercer sauntered out of the Windsor Hilton lobby in blue jeans and snakeskin boots. Stubble covered his chin and he was wearing dark sunglasses. A clip-on earring with a silver cross hung from his ear.

Mercer had driven the used Accord along I-94 to Detroit and had crossed the Ambassador Bridge to Windsor, Ontario. Once in Canada, he had dyed his hair from chestnut to sandy blond. Although he stood to gain great riches, he had tried to talk his friend out of stealing the *Colorado*.

He had expected Jake to fail and die, and when Jake had called him from the middle of the Atlantic Ocean, Mercer thought it had been the voice of a ghost. Worse, in his paranoia, he feared it might have been a federal agent simulating Jake's voice.

Thoughts of ghosts and paranoia vanished as Mercer reached a street corner payphone and called his bank.

Jake had trusted him to receive each Taiwanese payment into his account and then divvy up each accomplice's share. McKenzie, Bass, and Gant would each keep ten percent of the payments, Mercer twenty, and Jake fifty.

Mercer verified the latest payment.

"My account shows a deposit of forty million dollars, right?" he asked.

"Yes," said an operator with a European accent Mercer couldn't place.

Ten million down, and now forty more, he thought. *And we're only half way through.*

"Good," he said. "I'd like to make a few transfers to other accounts in your bank."

He pulled a sheet of paper from his breast pocket, unfolded it, and read the account number written next to the name 'McKenzie'.

"Four million to account number seven-three-two-four-four-nine dash seven-three-three."

He continued with four million dollar transfers for Gant and Bass. The last name on his list was Slate's.

I could keep Jake's twenty million for myself, he thought. *Shit, I bet I could still take back the twelve from the other guys.*

"Sir?" the operator asked.

"Yeah...hold on...I'm thinking," he said.

Greed is good, he thought. *But loyalty is better.*

He decided to let Jake have his money.

"Okay, let's transfer twenty million to fund number four-eight-eight-five-four dash seven-three-seven."

Mercer waited for the confirmation.

"That's it. Thank you," he said.

Okay, Jake, he thought, *I'm still with you.*

With intent of leaving his Honda behind, Mercer drove to a used car lot. As he stepped out of the Accord, a fat man with slick hair approached him.

"What are you looking for?" the beer-bellied salesman asked.

"Look, man, a buddy of mine saw my wife and some guy making out in this car last week. I've had troubles with that bitch before, and I don't want her getting this car in the divorce. It's in decent shape."

"Let me check her out," the fat salesman said.

As the salesman checked out the Accord, Mercer decided to post-pone the purchase of his next car. Better to clear his tracks by dumping his car here and getting the next one elsewhere.

"It's not in too bad shape," the salesman said. "I can take it. You want to use it as a trade in?"

"No," Mercer said. "I just want to put this nightmare behind me."

★

After paying American cash for a Ford Taurus on a second used car lot, Mercer drove along Route 401 toward Toronto. As the bleak sun backlit flat farmland, he reconsidered the dangerous role awaiting him if he continued to help Jake.

Signs indicated a handful of kilometers to Toronto, and Mercer faced a decision. He contemplated abandoning Jake for a life of inde-pendent wealth in Canada. He could continue to Montreal or even Quebec City, settle down, learn French, and enjoy his wealth. No one would find him.

As the off ramp for Route 400 north approached, Mercer remem-bered having promised Jake that he would go the distance. But by going the distance, Canada wouldn't be far enough away to hide.

Mercer swallowed, uttered a curse, and chose to keep his prom-ise. He turned onto Route 400 and pointed his Taurus at Ontario's sparsely populated regions. At the top of the Great Lakes, he would then double back west – and then north – en route to Alaska.

By turning onto Route 400, Mercer had committed. With one hundred sixty-four thousand dollars in American cash and thirty-eight hundred Canadian, Mercer headed down the slippery slope of no return.

★

In his stateroom, Brody spoke with the *Miami*'s executive officer.

"Pete, I need you to be ready to do me a favor."

"What's that sir?"

"You've been selected to command a submarine of your own soon. I'm considering letting you to take the *Miami* home as the acting commanding officer. I'm just about ready to pack it in."

"Captain?"

"I'm also annotating the deck log with your formal recommendation to open range to the *Colorado* before we were counter-detected."

"Sir, that annotation will do more harm to you than good for me. It's destructive."

"After letting the *Colorado* get away, my career's officially over. If I can turn my mistake into your advantage, then let's do it. You've learned a lot from me. My last lesson is to show you how to lose graciously."

★

Pacing in the Oval Office, Lance Ryder spoke with David Rankin, his National Security Advisor.

"Let's face it," Ryder said. "Admiral Mesher can pump all the sunshine up my ass that he wants, but we've had no contact with the *Colorado* for twenty-eight hours. It's gone and we've got a crisis. We need allied forces to help with this one."

"Sir, the implications of sharing this are too-"

"This could cost me the Presidency."

"It would destroy the nation's confidence. We can't afford that - not now - not with your neck sticking out in the Middle East. Not when you may have to pry the Chinese off of Taiwan."

"What other choice do I have?" Ryder asked.

"We can set up others to take the fall. Blame needs to go no higher than Admiral Mesher."

"If I go down, I go down with my integrity intact."

"But consider the nation," Rankin said. "You can't take this public without creating widespread panic, sir. There are options."

"What options?"

"We can get help secretly. I could leak this through intelligence channels and get allied resources to join us in the search. We should regain the *Colorado* when it passes through the Straits of Gibraltar. We can look for the warheads' radiation if they escape from the ship."

"Those options might work."

"We know that the *Colorado* is in the North Atlantic and probably heading toward Gibraltar, but the third party supporting this hijack doesn't know that we know. We need to retain that advantage. Silence and secrecy are your best options."

"Gather the Joint Chiefs, the DCI, and the Secretary of State to discuss using the intelligence channels," Ryder said. "We'll keep this quiet until I confer with them."

★

Four-foot swells rocked the chained network of three cargo containers under the eleven o'clock sun. The detonator in the top crate generated an electrical pulse. In unison, C-4 charges exploded and tore off the crate's door.

Attached to the plummeting steel door, a depth charge reached five hundred feet. Bellows sensors registered two hundred and twenty pounds per square inch of water pressure. The weapon exploded.

A shockwave shook the upper crate as water flowed into it and pushed the two buoys from the *Colorado* against its customized inner jail cell wall. As the inrush subsided, one buoy rose cleanly to the ocean's surface. The other bumped against the top of the crate prior to ascending. Having sensed immersion in water, the buoys reached the surface and transmitted a doomsday message that the USS *Colorado* had descended below crush depth.

As the buoys shrieked their message, the three crates descended below them. The metal walls of the remaining airtight crate groaned, creaked, and crumpled as the network of twisted metal plummeted to the ocean floor.

CHAPTER TWENTY-TWO

T HE TAIWANESE MINISTER OF DEFENSE sat before his top admirals and generals.

"Beijing has been enforcing an economic exclusive zone, a blockade in reality, against our inbound oil tankers and outbound military vessels. Their air assets have breached our defenses three times and have destroyed our major petroleum refineries. Although they supply refined gasoline and diesel fuel for an exorbitant price, the lack of jet fuel will soon cripple our air assets and half of our Navy."

Heads nodded somberly.

"With the sinking of three oil tankers inbound for Taipei and Kaoshiung, international insurance companies are withdrawing their assurance for major commercial vessels heading for our island. Diplomatic efforts have failed," he said.

Again heads nodded.

"I've decided that it's time for us to strike back."

Eyes around the table brightened.

"Before his departure, my French advisor drafted a plan that will destroy a major Chinese combatant."

"Where is the Frenchman?" a young admiral asked. "There has been concern that you take his counsel at the risk of rejecting that of your own military leaders."

The Minister had learned that the admiral, the youngest and most political of his flag officers, was spearheading a quiet insurgency within the Taiwanese military. The admiral sought to shift Taiwan from its defensive posture and retake its traditional offensive tone, concentrating forces and attacking coastal regions of mainland China.

The Minister considered the offensive stance idiotic. It would leave the island unguarded and give China justification to attempt amphibious landings, but the illogical fervor of the youth who supported it gave it life. To protect the island – and his career – the Minister counted on the shock value of his latest endeavor to hush the resistance.

"The Frenchman," the Minister said, "is presently on an operation."

The admiral frowned, and the Minister noticed that others at the table shared his displeasure.

"His last operation – the details of which you refuse to share with us - failed in anything but inciting the mainland to accelerate its blockade," the admiral said.

"His last operation identified one of my deputies as a mole," the Minister said. "And with that discovery, we will use one of the communication channels that we believe the mole compromised as a way to set a trap."

"A trap?" the admiral asked and smirked.

"We will make the mainland believe that we are trying to sneak American weapons through their blockade. They will send a combatant to investigate, and that will be their mistake. Our stealth vessel, the *Tai Chiang*, will destroy the Chinese combatant."

The admiral became agitated.

"Sir," he said, "the *Tai Chiang* is the first ship of its class, and weapon system integration problems are delaying its deployment. The ship has no missiles. Engineers are working on the problem, but it's not ready to attack a major combatant. And even if it were, it is not designed to exchange blows with larger warships."

"It has its stealth and torpedoes, does it not?"

"Yes, sir, but–"

"Then you will read the details of the operation left behind by the Frenchman and make the preparations."

"Sir," the admiral said. "I will follow orders, of course, but I must question the use of the *Tai Chiang*. We have frigates capable of major engagement. Why not mass them together with air power and strike-"

The Minister stood and silence enveloped the room.

"I have chosen the *Tai Chiang* because this is a two-part mission," he said. "The *Tai Chiang* will destroy a major combatant and serve as our first step in shattering the Chinese mainland's resolve in enforcing the blockade.

"Once that is accomplished, we will claim that the *Tai Chiang* was lost in the exchange, but in reality, it will employ its stealth to continue north for refueling and weapons reload at a secret location in Japan."

Any disdain for the plan once evident in his admiral's face had vanished. The Minister appeared to have piqued his curiosity. "For what purpose?" the admiral asked.

"The *Tai Chiang* will serve as a delivery vessel for nuclear weapons," the Minister said.

All eyes at the table opened wide.

"You will all dedicate your assets," the Minister said, "to ensure that the stealth vessel *Tai Chiang* passes through the Chinese blockade unnoticed so that it can retrieve and return with the warheads. The operation could last up to two months, and until the *Tai Chiang* succeeds, we never speak of this outside this room."

The admiral struggled to voice a whisper.

"How can this be, sir?" he asked.

"Read the Frenchman's operational plan, and you will understand everything you need to know."

★

Through his facemask, Taiwanese Sergeant Yangi Zhao watched sunlight fade into the depths of the Western Pacific Ocean. Zhao both lamented and savored that he would soon give life to the abyss.

By feeling opposing emotions, the Taiwanese commando achieved the neutrality he would need to carry out Renard's plan, Operation *Northern Star*.

The shaking of the cargo ship *Northern Star* rumbled through Zhao's head as its propellers churned backwards. The ship halted. Zhao unhooked the steel cable that connected him to the ship's ladder rungs below the water's surface. He bit his rebreather mouthpiece, drew recycled air, and waited.

Ten minutes earlier, the *Northern Star's* radar had picked up a vessel approaching at thirty-four knots. Reacting to the anticipated warship, Sergeant Zhao and his partner, Corporal Wu, had slipped into the water as the *Northern Star* slowed.

Renard's trap was set.

Per Renard's plan, a bogus Taiwanese message had been broadcast stating that the *Northern Star* carried American Harpoon Block IIB anti-ship/land attack missiles to Taiwan. The message was broadcast with encryption codes compromised by the traitor who had foiled Renard's theft.

Rung by rung, Zhao pushed himself to join Corporal Wu in the concealing depths. He tugged at an eyehook between Wu's shoulders to ensure that it held a mesh knapsack carrying military plastic C-4 explosives.

He heard the smooth swish of machined propeller screws as a moving wall eclipsed waterborne sunbeams. He calculated that the warship's length spanned one hundred and thirty meters.

A Luda class destroyer, he thought. *Its crew will board us and search for Harpoon Missiles but will depart empty-handed – except for my explosives.*

He reviewed his mental schematic of the *Luda* class and plotted where he would strap charges to the warship's propeller bearings.

Zhao's charges would not sink the compartmentalized warship. But placed on its propeller bearings, they would cripple the destroyer for someone else to finish the job.

★

Over the *Northern Star's* horizon, electromagnetic waves from an ocean full of radar systems tickled the Taiwanese patrol ship, *Tai Chiang*.

The *Tai Chiang's* skin, a thin layer of radar-absorbent synthetic rubber stretched over Kevlar-plated armor, diffused the radar energy.

With a low profile and few sharp edges, the *Tai Chiang* became invisible to radar.

The *Tai Chiang* resembled an F-117 stealth jet cockpit rising from a tapered spearhead. Zigzag tiger stripes of varying grays camouflaged the ship, and shaded bridge windows made it a menacing image.

★

Lieutenant Commander Lin Jin-Zhu, the son of a Taipei banker, commanded the *Tai Chiang*. He walked with a swagger. Ten years of proving his tactical skills had earned him command of Taiwan's most capable vessel.

Four men joined Lin in comprising the *Tai Chiang's* bridge battle complement. On either bridge wing, a lookout scanned the ocean through binoculars. Two junior officers sat at battle control stations behind him.

For our first time in combat, I will control all systems, he thought. *I do not need the errors of inexperienced men undermining my actions.*

Lin strapped himself into his chair. Donning a headset, he studied the monitors of the ship's primary battle control station. He touched a pad and brought up the ship's sensor, propulsion, and weapons displays.

He studied the propulsion sound-level display. Two gas turbines, shock-mounted and quieted by active sound nullifiers, emanated imperceptible noise. Any listening vessel would fail to hear the *Tai Chiang*.

Other displays revealed the *Tai Chiang's* thermal stealth. Hot gases from the turbines mixed with water ejected from the ship's rear. The remaining exhaust heat preheated the incoming air that fed the turbines. Thus, the *Tai Chiang* was dark to infrared, inaudible, and invisible.

A window on Lin's sensor screen annotated that the signal strength of the Eye Shield radar from the Chinese *Luda* class destroyer, *Hefei*, posed no threat.

He watched the bearing – the geographic direction as measured from the *Tai Chiang* - to the *Hefei's* Eye Shield radar separate from the *Northern Star's* commercial Okean radar. The *Hefei* was running away.

Lin examined the weapons he would wield against the *Hefei*. All systems were ready except the Hsiung Feng III anti-ship missiles.

He had been disappointed to learn that the missile's prototypes had flown into the ground during testing, but Renard's plan didn't need them. It required only the *Tai Chiang's* stealth, Sergeant Zhao's explosives, and specialized torpedoes.

Lin had agreed to let engineers alter the ship's torpedoes to run at twenty-eight knots, slowing them but maximizing their ranges to eleven miles so that the *Tai Chiang* could strike from a distance.

He depressed a button on his battle control station keypad and spoke through the headset to his executive officer, Lieutenant Yang Kai-huang, in the ship's auxiliary bridge below. Lin had no respect for Yang, the son of a machinist who had used the Navy to climb above his class.

"Yang, this is real combat. If you second-guess me, I will cast you over the side myself."

Lin tapped a button that shifted his voice to the entire crew.

"I estimate that the target has made forty knots since leaving the *Northern Star*. We will head north to parallel its course. I will control propulsion, weapons, and sensors from my battle control station. It is time to hunt our prey."

Lin accelerated the *Tai Chiang* to fifty-one knots. A display at his battle control station revealed that dual magnetic drive units ionized incoming seawater, polarized it, and spewed it outward to thrust the *Tai Chiang* on a parallel course with the *Hefei*.

Lin listened as the *Tai Chiang* intercepted radio traffic from the *Hefei*. A tense sailor gave a damage report to Chinese East Fleet head-quarters.

"*...series of explosions...under attack...possible sabotage...propulsion shafts vibrating out of control...loss of propulsion...dead in the water...*"

Dead in the water, Lin thought. *Sergeant Zhao placed his charges well.*

He turned the *Tai Chiang* toward the *Hefei*.

"Superstructure is visible. Light smoke rising from target," a look-out said from the bridge wing.

Using the height of the *Hefei* and trigonometry, Lin calculated a distance of fourteen miles to his target. The *Tai Chiang's* infrared sensors verified his estimate. Three more miles to torpedo range.

"I can see the bridge," the lookout said.

Lin's finger caressed the torpedo release. Despite facing a fully armed destroyer, he would make sure his weapons hit. He stayed his course.

Ten and a half miles, his display read. Ten and a quarter. A red light flashed and an alarm whined.

"Wasp Head gunfire control!" he said. "We've been discovered. Jamming with Chang-Feng electronic countermeasures. Raising Sea Chaparral air defense missile launchers."

He looked over his shoulder and watched a twin-rail launcher rise on the *Tai Chiang's* fantail.

"Within launch range. Slowing the ship," he said.

Lin tapped an all stop key and watched his battle control station display. An electromagnetic field in the engine room collapsed, and water coasted through parallel propulsion flow paths. Two beach-ball-sized valves rotated shut and cut off the seawater flow.

"Back full," Lin said and tapped his controls.

A pair of booster pumps in the engine room sucked water from behind the *Tai Chiang* and pulled fluid backwards through the magnetic drive units. Reverse electric coils energized, polarizing and charging the reverse-flowing water. Hydraulic fluid reopened the ball-valves, letting water suck the *Tai Chiang* backwards.

Nine miles from the *Hefei*, the *Tai Chiang* shook as it slowed. Through his touch pad, Lin ordered each torpedo launcher to slide outward, but a warning light flashed.

"Damn! Low hydraulic pressure."

Lin idled the port torpedo nest. Waning hydraulic pressure inched the starboard nest outward.

He hit all three starboard launch keys. Bridge windows shuddered as compressed gases spat torpedoes into the ocean. Three weapons swam toward the idled destroyer at twenty-eight knots.

"Starboard torpedoes away," he said and sneered.

"Normal launch, torpedoes clear," a lookout said.

"Ahead flank. Left twenty degrees twist," Lin said.

The magnetic drive system thrust the ship forward. Bow thrusters shot water sideways to push the ship to its left. The *Tai Chiang* leaned hard over.

Lin's infrared display alarmed when it identified rocket contrails from the *Hefei's* six HY-2 anti-ship missiles. Heat signatures revealed that the missiles were racing toward the *Tai Chiang* at Mach 0.9.

Lin swiveled the ship's forward-mounted seventy-six millimeter cannon as quickly as the hydraulic plant could support and energized all radar systems. His Marconi radar painted the HY-2 missiles, fed the data to the central computers, and calculated optimal use of the *Tai Chiang's* defenses.

He unloaded his four retrofitted American Standard anti-air missiles from the Sea Chaparral launcher. They shot from their launchers and accelerated to Mach 4.5.

Standard warheads sliced through three of the incoming HY-2's in a fireworks display. Smoke plumes billowing above the water traced the paths of splintered missiles. The fourth Standard locked onto shrapnel and missed its target.

Lin monitored battle screens showing that the remaining three HY-2's were chasing him at eight miles per minute. A computer display recognized the search pattern of the incoming weapons and recommended that two chaff canisters be expended.

Lin depressed a button. Pressurized canisters on the bridge wing popped open and belched metallic shards. Lin circled the *Tai Chiang* back underneath the blossoming cloud of metal. Snuffed by the metallic blizzard, his radar screens became intermittent fuzziness.

He ordered the Chang Feng ECM system to jam the incoming HY-2 missiles' seekers but saw no effect. He refocused his jamming energy onto a solitary missile, and it spiraled into the water.

As the cannon steadied, Lin commanded it to attack the two remaining incoming missiles. Flashes erupted as each pump of the muzzle shook bridge windows. On Lin's battle control station, the closest HY-2 missile disappeared as a fused proximity round exploded and crumpled its fuselage.

The final incoming missile passed through the chaff cloud over the *Tai Chiang*. It circled and attacked the chaff three times before exhausting its fuel and splashing into the sea.

Lin turned the *Tai Chiang's* computer to jamming the *Hefei's* gun control radars. Five-inch shells from the destroyer dropped far from the *Tai Chiang*, and Lin knew the *Hefei's* counterattack would be short lived.

In the distance, three explosions rocked the *Hefei*. The ocean erupted around the destroyer. As it settled, the ship listed.

Lin drove the *Tai Chiang* back into range and launched the three port-side torpedoes to finish the job. The *Hefei* sank in less than ten minutes. Only a few lifeboats dotted the water.

Lin remembered his father boasting about ice water in the veins helping him outmaneuver people on opposing sides of transactions. He inhaled, sensed his slow pulse, and realized that he was his father's son.

CHAPTER TWENTY-THREE

"WHAT DO THOSE BUOYS INDICATE?" President Ryder asked.

"They're launched from a Trident submarine to indicate that it has sunk. A sensor sets them off when the ship descends below crush depth," Admiral Mesher said.

"You're sure it's the *Colorado*?"

"The buoys are submarine-specific."

"It can't be faked?"

"Impossible. The frequencies are top secret and scrambled."

"I mean the sinking. Could that be faked?"

"Unlikely. The warhead explosion and the implosion of an airtight compartment indicate that the *Colorado* was destroyed. We'll be running the acoustic tapes through the Johns Hopkins Oceanic Research labs, but all evidence indicates that the *Colorado* is on the bottom."

"How long until we find the wreckage?"

"This was in the same depth of water as the *Titanic*," Mesher said. "It could take months."

"Okay, let's assume for the moment that the *Colorado* was sunk. Who sank it and why?"

"It's possible that Lieutenant Slate accidentally shot himself with his own torpedo," Mesher said.

"Who the hell was he shooting at? Us?"

"Doubtful, sir. We would've heard him. I'm just offering theories."

"Keep going."

"It's possible that a torpedo detonated in its tube."

"How likely is that?"

"Unlikely."

"You're not building a good case."

"There's also the possibility that a foreign vessel penetrated our escort perimeter and sank the *Colorado*."

"Admiral, the nation is breathing down my neck about that Trident. If you were in my shoes, would you say that the *Colorado* is on the bottom of the Atlantic?"

"I can't speculate further until more evidence becomes available."

"Give me your gut feel."

"Mister President, this is like being blindfolded and shooting a shouting man. You don't know if you've hit your target until you hear silence. Even then you may not be certain who you hit, if anyone. But based upon the data we have now, the *Colorado* was destroyed."

★

In the privacy of his stateroom, John Brody swallowed his fourth shot of Jack Daniels. His mind danced with demons.

Carole Brody lay in bed. Her naked body invited the touch of a stranger. Her brow furrowed as she faced Brody.

"Failure!" she said.

The image disintegrated.

A new image crept into his head.

Towering over a group of officers, Slate's commanding officer, Commander Thomas Henry, approached a podium. He accepted his appointment to admiral and spoke into a microphone.

"I accept this promotion as the token nigger admiral because John Brody was too stupid to sell out. Hey John, you didn't even make captain, did you?"

"Fuck it," Brody said. "After Jake stole your submarine, your career's going down with mine."

Next image.

Standing on the bridge of the USS *Colorado*, Jake studied the seas as wind blew his hair. He grinned.

"Hey, John. How are you doing?" he asked. "Were you the dip-shit I just outsmarted?"

"Fuck it," Brody said and slammed a fifth shot. Another shot later, he was crying over a picture of his wife. Then he wiped his eyes and studied his face in the mirror. He saw nothing he respected.

Desperate to feel an iota of dignity, he grabbed his bottle of whiskey and emptied it into his toilet.

★

The next morning, Brody felt dehydrated and queasy as he addressed the *Miami*'s officers.

"I expect that in a few days, the Commodore will let us come home. I'm going to let Pete Parks run the show. I just wanted to thank you guys for being the best wardroom a skipper could have."

While sad faces remained somber, the wardroom door opened. The short, stocky image of Senior Chief Schmidt, Brody's sonar technician, scratched his grayish brown mustache while reporting in a gritty baritone.

"Captain, you told me to let you know if I found something."

"Yeah?"

"I found something."

Brody followed Schmidt up the stairs to the sonar room. Stinking of body odor and grime, the sonar technician huddled over an audio machine.

"I think you're right about the *Colorado*, Captain."

"I had a feeling this guy was too good to get sunk," Brody said. "What do you have?"

"There's no doubt a warhead exploded under where they found the *Colorado*'s buoys. What bothers me is the implosion of the hull."

"Go on."

"Well, sir. First of all, the *Colorado* has four compartments, if you count the reactor compartment. Most likely we'd have heard several compartments implode, but we only heard one."

"The compartments could have equalized pressure on the way down."

"That's possible, but what I really don't like is the timing. The *Colorado*'s sinking seemed fast, so I listened with a stopwatch. The hull imploded twenty-one seconds after the explosion. That's too quick."

"Maybe the *Colorado* was deep when it was struck."

"Still, sir," Schmidt said, "there's one important thing missing - the creaking. I don't have to tell you that high-yield steel puts up a good fight, but we had only twelve seconds of catastrophic creaking before the pop."

"That doesn't make sense, Senior."

"That's my point, sir. I already had two other guys check the timing and my logic. Something exploded and something sank, and the *Colorado*'s doomsday buoys were found on top of it all. But it doesn't compute."

"Okay, Senior. Let's get the officers and sonar team together. We're all going to listen to this tape."

★

Jake popped Brussels sprouts into his mouth while he watched the Frenchman swivel the periscope.

"How's it going?" he asked.

"I just returned from the navigation center with a GPS fix," Renard said. "Our gyroscopic navigators are tracking. Scott is raising the radio mast. You could save us time at periscope depth by handling the radio download for me."

"No problem. Are we alone?"

"Nothing on sonar or visual," Renard said. "No ESM. I never thought I would enjoy such isolation."

Jake placed his microwaved bowl of canned sprouts on a counter and flipped switches to align the radio antenna.

He listened to the whir of a radio transceiver as it accepted a download. Then he walked from the module and lifted a microphone to his mouth.

"Mister Renard, I've got the transmission," Jake said. "Lower the radio mast and take us deep."

Jake popped the last sprout into his mouth as he ripped off the printout. Reading as he walked uphill against the ship's diving angle, he returned to the control room.

"Sweet!" he said.

McKenzie, Renard, and Tiger turned to listen as Jake read aloud.

"At a press conference today, President Lance Ryder stated that the USS *Colorado*, underway under suspicious circumstances since May 11th, was sunk at sea two days ago. He will not confirm details of the situation, but sources state that a reactor accident-"

"Thank God. Now, no one will be chasing us," McKenzie said.

"Congratulations, Jake," Renard said. "Your maneuver with the *Custom Venture* worked perfectly. I cannot help but think that you're charmed. However, we need to keep our wits about us. That statement by your president could be a deception in its own right."

"Maybe, but I think it's safe to speed up."

"Agreed," Renard said.

"I don't know about this fairwater damage, though. What do you think about nine knots – at least until we're under the ice?"

"Nine knots will add almost a week to our journey versus our planned speed of twelve," Renard said.

"I planned leeway into the timing. I don't think Taiwan will mind waiting," Jake said.

"That may depend. How is the situation there?"

Jake scanned the news report. A blurb on the subject followed a story about a Middle East terrorist group bombing a London subway.

"China lost a destroyer during an exchange with an unnamed Taiwanese combatant in the Western Pacific, but the Taiwanese combatant had to be scuttled at sea," Jake said. "Then there's something about Chinese submarine attacks against oil tankers inbound to Taiwan and insurance companies refusing to cover Taiwanese commercial vessels."

"It's as I'd feared. The mainland stranglehold is in place, and even as it resists, the Taiwanese fleet is too small and can ill afford one-for-one exchanges. If this journey takes too long, Taiwan may not be around to receive the warheads."

★

"Our doubts about the *Colorado* sinking reached the CNO," Brody said. "He's skeptical, but he's sent the *Boise* and the *Philly* to look for the *Colorado* in the Gibraltar shipping lanes. The extra P-3's are standing down - and so are we."

"Forgive me sir," Parks, his executive officer, said in a drawl, "but the *Colorado* was your battle, and you're the one who discovered that it might be alive. Why do other people get to chase him? It isn't right."

"The Squadron Commodore did me a little favor, Pete. He got Sublant to let me stay out four extra weeks with any patrol area I request. We get any water we want outside of allied submarine patrol areas."

"Really? What did you have in mind, sir?"

"If the *Colorado* is alive and going where we all thought it was, then Slate gets eaten alive before Gibraltar."

"He wouldn't have a chance in hell, sir."

"So let's assume that the *Colorado* is alive and heading someplace besides the Mediterranean. If Slate is sly enough to fake a Trident's death, then he's smart enough to change direction on us."

"I follow you, sir, but the world is a big place."

"I wouldn't put it beyond him to think he can shoot between Greenland and Iceland, or between Iceland and the United Kingdom, without being heard."

"At least six nations patrol the G-I-UK Gap, sir, and they have hydrophones strung across the ocean floor from Greenland to France."

Parks inhaled through his nostrils, but Brody had masked his hangover breath with a mint. After dumping his whisky, Brody thought, it would be the last time on the *Miami* he'd have to worry about it.

"But if no one is looking," Brody said, "then the G-I-UK Gap becomes possible for a Trident, don't you think?"

"I'll buy that, sir. But why the Gap? There's no place to go up there, except NATO nations and Russia."

"Unless he's going for the polar ice cap."

"It's never been done by a Trident, sir."

"Slate's brilliant. Heck, he's got us so turned around we don't even know if he's alive. I wouldn't put an under-ice passage beyond him."

★

As Grant Mercer stepped into a waterfront bar in Nome, Alaska, a heavyset native bartender eyed him.

"Where're you from, son?" the man asked.

"I travel a lot," Mercer said.

"You don't look like a hunter or a tourist. What brings you here?"

"I need a boat," Mercer said. "Something that can survive open ocean and hold supplies for four men for two weeks. Something that can make around twenty knots."

"You're asking a lot. What do you need it for?"

"I'm with the Natural Resources Defense Council," Mercer said. "Three of my associates are going to join me with sonar equipment to spy on the U.S. Navy. They're testing low frequency active sonar systems, but they're breaking the law. And they're deafening whales."

"Deafening whales?"

Mercer never understood the fuss about dolphins and tuna in humanity's effort to feed itself and struggled to feign indignation.

"It's very serious. And it's not just whales, but they get the worst of it. The Navy is bombarding marine life with noise levels millions of times stronger than rock concerts. Do you know what that does to whales? It kills them, that's what it does. They stop eating, they stop mating, they stop migrating. That's a tragedy I hope to prevent," Mercer said.

"I had no idea."

"Few people do. But my team's going to catch the Navy in the act."

"Last year's fishing season was real bad," the man said. "I know a few guys who are selling."

CHAPTER TWENTY-FOUR

Sᴇʀɢᴇᴀɴᴛ Kᴀᴏ Yᴀᴛ-sᴇɴ, ᴛʜᴇ Tᴀɪᴡᴀɴᴇsᴇ veteran leading half a dozen young commandos aboard the *Colorado* on his nation's greatest mission, stared at a stone image in the mirror. His skin looked worn, his eyes hollow. Time had cut lines into his face, as did the pain he hid behind it.

As Kao leaned forward, he felt the grating burn of arthritis in the vertebrae broken in a parachuting accident decades ago. Raising a toothbrush to his mouth, he could feel the sting in a shoulder long ago dislocated by a premature C-4 charge detonation.

Pain reminded him of mortality, but he did not fear death. He accepted that the odds favored him dying on the *Colorado*, and he knew he would not be the only casualty.

He replayed in his mind a meeting he had had with the Minister of Defense and a most offensive Lieutenant Commander Lin, the commanding officer of the Taiwanese stealth patrol craft, *Tai Chiang*.

The meeting had taken place weeks earlier, but it had affected Kao so intensely that it still played through his mind.

Pierre Renard, the Minister's trusted advisor, had just outlined a plan to steal American nuclear weapons. Kao, the Minister, and Commander Lin had had to modify the Frenchman's plan, but they had found it workable. Renard had just departed, and charts marking key events in the plan to steal the *Colorado* still covered the table.

Sergeant Kao watched the *Tai Chiang's* commanding officer glare at the aging and stressed Minister.

"Sir, what are you paying this man?" Lin asked.

The question's aggressiveness startled Kao.

"I know of your father, Lin," the Minister said. "He is a powerful man in the financial world. I'm sure he trained you to think of financial risk and reward."

"Indeed," Lin said.

"The total price is one hundred and twenty million U.S. dollars," the Minister said. "I have paid ten percent already. I will pay an additional forty percent when Kao informs me that he has control of the submarine in the Atlantic Ocean, and the rest once the weapons are aboard your ship."

"Sir, the remaining one hundred and eight million U.S. dollars would be better spent smuggling jet fuel to the island," Lin said.

"The payments are trivial compared to the reward."

"But unnecessary. The Frenchman can command the ship. Why not kill the Americans once the submarine is at sea?"

Kao had seen brashness in the younger officers, but nothing as bold as challenging the top man in the military. He could no longer hold his tongue.

"I do not take killing lightly," he said.

"And I cannot default on payments and expect results," the Minister said.

"Then we can conserve half of our investment," Lin said. "When my ship approaches the submarine for the rendezvous, Kao's team can neutralize the Americans. And why not the Frenchman as well? This will enable us to save sixty million dollars and prevent five men from escaping with knowledge of this operation."

"I value the Frenchman," the Minister said. "He has already proven his worth by identifying a mole and enabling us to set this trap with your ship."

"That was made possible by circumstances we shall not see again. The Frenchman is overvalued," Lin said.

"Do not tell me how to value assets!"

Kao foresaw a showdown that his stressed Minister could ill afford. He wanted to silence the patrol craft's commander with a knife, but he played peacemaker.

"I could make a judgment call," Kao said. "I will understand the temperament of the men on that ship and will be able to judge the risk. I will place the situation under control prior to docking with the *Tai Chiang*."

"Yes, very well," the Minister said. "Kao will have final control over the fate of the Americans, but I want Renard returned to me as my advisor. Am I clear?"

Lin had ignored the Minister and met Kao's glare.

"Kao makes the call on the Americans. The Frenchman returns. Am I clear?" the Minister said again.

"Perfectly," Lin said, sneering.

As Kao marched through the teakwood lined passageway leading from the Minister's antechamber, he heard the clap of Lin's heels against the marble floor behind him. Kao wanted nothing to do with the commander of the *Tai Chiang* and outpaced him.

"Sergeant Kao!" Lin said.

Kao stopped.

"You do not approve of my ways?" Lin asked.

"I am in no position to pass judgment, sir."

"Yet you do."

Kao remained silent.

"You think I am overstepping my bounds, but you are wrong," Lin said. "The Minister is poising us for failure, and I am not alone in this judgment. Many unit commanders believe that we have the superior forces necessary to overcome our lack of numbers. We must strike – offensively - while we have the resources. When the Minister's strategy of endurance fails, there will be a movement to replace him."

"Why are you telling me this?" Kao asked.

"I do not approve of this mission. I should be staying here to defend the island, not slinking across the ocean."

"You mean stay here and advance your career in front of the admiralty," Kao said.

"Be careful, Sergeant. You may not be in the Navy, but I can still bring disciplinary action upon you."

"I was out of line, sir."

Lin ignored the insincerity. "If by chance you're still alive in two months and manage to bring the *Colorado* where I can get to it, make no mistake that I will see this mission succeed."

"It is fortunate that your personal aspirations correspond with your duties...at least at the moment."

Lin laughed through his nose.

"Not all men follow orders blindly. As long as I am taking part in this mission and you come through on your end, I will get my warheads."

"Then may I assume you have said all you wish?"

"Only one more thing, Sergeant – just to be clear. I do not care what the Minister says. I will not tolerate having the Americans or the Frenchman control our destiny."

Those final words continued to echo in Kao's mind.

He realized that if he left the westerners alive, Lin would act. Once the warheads were transferred to his ship, the brazen commander of the *Tai Chiang* could send the *Colorado* a parting torpedo just to kill them, and the explosion could destroy the secrecy of the entire mission.

He wrestled with his decision, but in light of Commander Lin's demeanor, Kao could envision no scenario that preserved the lives of his American shipmates. If the *Colorado* reached the *Tai Chiang*, Kao would order his team to kill the Americans once the stealth vessel was in sight.

As for the Frenchman, his fate seemed murky. The Minister had ordered Renard returned to his side, but Kao doubted that Commander Lin would let Renard live. Nevertheless, he would wait to decide the Frenchman's fate. But the Americans were dead men.

Accepting his decision, he maneuvered the bristles across his teeth and spat. He shifted his weight and felt a surgically reattached tendon grate across his patella. Pain shot through the commando's body, but the image in the mirror remained stone.

CHAPTER TWENTY-FIVE

MAY 31, 2006
MARGINAL ICE ZONE, ARCTIC OCEAN:

AFTER TEN DAYS OF TRANSIT, Brody slowed the *Miami* to navigate around icebergs. A sailor in the control room announced that the high frequency sonar measured twenty feet between the *Miami's* sail and the wall of ice above.

Brody glanced at a depth gauge with numbers that had been shrinking during the days he drove north into shallower waters. The seafloor and iceberg squeezed the *Miami*, but Brody felt comfortable going deeper.

"Make your depth three hundred feet," he said.

The sonar display showed clear water above as the iceberg drifted over and behind the *Miami*.

As a junior officer on an older submarine, Brody had patrolled the under-ice world. As he approached it again, he felt a chill. He remembered that the polar world forgave no mistakes – neither those of navigation nor those of battle.

He wondered if he could pull the trigger on his friend and protégé.

Ordered to trail Jake, then ordered to kill him, he had no official guidance on what to do if he found him. He had to set his own rules.

Jake had once been a friend, he thought, but that no longer mattered. He had committed mutiny, placed national security at risk, and had even launched a live weapon at the *Miami*.

If he found him, Brody decided, he would send Jake to an arctic grave.

★

"We're clearing the marginal ice zone, Captain," Senior Chief Schmidt said. "Background noise is falling off, and it's quiet ahead. We're going under the ice cap."

"Good call, Senior," Brody said. "Agrees with the navigation officer's fix."

"The glacier's pretty far south this year," Schmidt said. "All that ice breaking off is hard on the ears, you know. Now it gets quieter. Instead of my ears hurting from all the noise, I have to start listening for a pin to drop from a hundred miles away."

"A pin to drop or a Trident submarine to slip by," Brody said. "I don't know if the *Colorado*'s here yet or if it's even coming, but start listening for her. Even up here, she can come and go in the blink of an eye."

★

Mike Gant's voice shot out over a loudspeaker and awoke Jake. He had been dreaming about his revenge coming to fruition at Commander Thomas Henry's conviction at a Court Martial.

"Smoke in the feed bay," Gant said. "I dumped all AC buses."

Half asleep, Jake marched through the shadows cast by emergency lighting. Buzzers behind darkened control panels rang in his ears during his walk to the *Colorado*'s engine room. As he reached the ship's lowest propulsion plant caverns, he smelled burning rubber and saw floating wisps of gray.

Two commandos held battery-operated battle lanterns over David Bass's rotund body as he studied the motor controller circuitry to the port patrol feed pump. Jake gazed around the electrician at charred wires.

"Looks like over-current," Bass said.

"Low grounds?" Jake asked.

"Probably. Nobody's keeping things clean, so carbon dust is building up. It's only a matter of time before dust connects everything to grounded metal. Shit's going to keep shorting out."

"Let's fix this problem first and worry about the rest of the ship later. Isolate the motor controller from the electrical bus and then come back to maneuvering. We have a reactor to start. It scrammed on interlock when Gant dumped all the electrical buses, so everything's still hot. It should go fast."

After reassuring Gant of his decision to extinguish the *Colorado's* electricity in response to the errant bus voltages caused by the dying pump, Jake led an uneventful reactor warm restart.

With his reactor back online, Jake steamed the *Colorado* northeast at nine knots. He traversed the G-I-UK Gap. With no one looking for the Trident in the gap, he passed without a trace. Jake kept the *Colorado* on its northerly trek deep enough to pass under most icebergs and fortunate enough to not bump into the rest.

It was nineteen days after faking the Trident's death before Jake slowed the *Colorado* so that it crawled at five knots into the quiet, surreal world of the polar ice cap.

Inside his Trident Missile submarine under the ice, Jake huddled with Renard over a chart in the control room.

"The chart is accurate, Jake?"

"As good as it gets up here. This is not the quickest route, but it's the one adjusted best for the magnetic and gravitational deviations on the gyroscopes."

"Indeed," Renard said. "The question of location becomes tricky. In these latitudes, magnetic north is no longer just a few degrees from true north. It lies on its unique, constantly changing direction, rendering our compasses useless. And with ice overhead, GPS fixes are elusive. We're completely reliant on inertial navigators."

"Even those are less accurate up here," Jake said. "But if we go slow and follow this charted path, we can use the fathometer to at least verify we're close to the right place based upon water depth."

"I concur with our path, but I'm still concerned about ridges."

"We just have to watch out for them and go slow. If we go bump at five knots, nothing's going to breach the pressure hull. We'll have dry racks all the way to the Pacific."

★

Brody watched Senior Chief Schmidt sip coffee, rub his eyes, and gaze at green static on the narrowband frequency display. Brody wondered what Schmidt saw and stared at a green fuzzy line rising on the monitor. It seemed no more than static to Brody.

Schmidt flipped a trackball with the index finger of one hand and slipped a headset over his ears with the other. He lowered his head and closed his eyes. Brody was bursting with curiosity but let Schmidt battle in silence to discern real noise from sonic hallucinations and memories.

"It's the scraping noise of a Trident submarine's distillate brine pump," Schmidt said. "Captain, this is the *Colorado*."

"I'll be damned," Brody said. "We just found a ghost."

"Sir, we should try to penetrate the ice and tell someone he's alive. And maybe we can get some clear orders about whether we're supposed to trail him or take him out."

"No, he'd hear us, and it could take us ten tries to break through. I don't want to risk it. We'd lose him again before we could tell anyone."

"So what do you want to do, sir?"

"The President told the world that the *Colorado* was destroyed. Orders or not, I'm going to prove him right."

★

For thirty-six hours the *Miami* closed distance on the *Colorado*, crossing behind its baffles and passing to its far side. The change in the geometry enabled Brody to trace out the Trident's path. The targeting solution tightened as he moved in for the kill.

He felt that he was living an out-of-body experience. Someone else, his coldhearted clone, was commanding the *Miami* to kill Jake.

"Shoot tube one!" he said.

His ears popped as high-pressure air thrust an Advanced Capability ADCAP torpedo into the Arctic Ocean.

★

High-pitched chimes from the *Colorado's* torpedo alarm paralyzed Renard.

"Shit! Torpedo!" McKenzie said.

"Arctic tactics," Renard said. "We're going to the roof."

"We can't break through!" McKenzie said.

"Do as I say," Renard said. "Mister Tiger, rudder amidships. Order a full backing bell."

Renard grabbed a microphone.

"Torpedo in the water," he said. "Stop the ship."

The ship shuddered. Renard thought of the children he and Marie would never have.

"Torpedo? Why the fuck are we stopping?" Bass asked over the circuit.

"Follow my orders!" Renard said.

He joined McKenzie by the ship's control panel.

"I need your help," Renard said. "Get us to the roof and keep us there."

His face puffy with sleep, Jake sprang into the control room wearing underwear and a tee-shirt.

"Why are we at all stop?" Jake asked.

"We cannot outrun a torpedo. I've started an ice picking maneuver."

"Bullshit! We need speed," Jake said and reached for the circuit.

"No, Jake! I assure you this is the proper under-ice tactic. Trust me!"

Jake gazed in silence.

"By the time we could achieve evasion speed," Renard said, "it would be too late."

Jake flipped a switch to silence the torpedo alarm chimes.

"No bearing change," Jake said. "Coming straight for us. Frequency's American."

"Even an American torpedo can be fooled, Jake."

"An ice pick, huh? Let's do it right, then. We're going dead silent."

Jake's confidence gave Renard a glimmer of hope that he would see Marie again.

"Scott," Jake said, "head below and de-energize the four-hundred-hertz machines. Silence alarms on the way down."

"Scram the plant," Jake said over the circuit. "Dump all buses. We're going super quiet. Brace for impact."

Darkness enshrouded the control room. The deep swish of cooling fans faded. Renard watched dim emergency bulbs backlight Jake as he ran around the room silencing battery-powered buzzers.

Renard's stomach dropped as the *Colorado's* sail struck the ice. He grasped a railing for support. A shock wave jostled his bones, and the deck plates rolled underfoot.

Technical manuals hit the deck and pencils rolled off the navigation table. Staring forty degrees down at the opposite wall, Renard realized that the *Colorado's* sail acted as a fulcrum against the ice.

At least the ship had reached the roof, he thought. He had a chance to survive, provided his aging mind had remembered the correct arctic tactic.

★

The seeker of the *Miami's* ADCAP torpedo transmitted a thirty-two-kilohertz acoustic signal. The seeker heard its return bouncing off an inverted ice ridge. It transmitted again to verify the target. Then a third time.

Convinced it had found a target, the weapon followed its under-ice protocols. It ceased transmitting and listened but heard no mechanical noises. It accelerated toward the ridge, slowed, and listened again.

It heard ice buckling under glacial pressures – the creaking, the snapping, and the echoes from the shallow sea floor - but nothing it classified as mechanical.

The ADCAP torpedo concluded that the ridge was not a submarine. It re-energized its active seeker and raced toward the expected location of the *Colorado*.

The ADCAP seeker detected its sonic return from the *Colorado's* hull. It slowed and listened, but it heard creaking that it identified as shifting ice. Hearing no mechanical frequencies, the torpedo continued under the *Colorado*.

The torpedo circled back, re-identified the Trident as part of the natural world, ran out of fuel, and sank.

★

"Where's our torpedo, executive officer?" Brody asked.

"It's circled back and shut down, sir," Parks said. "No sign of the *Colorado*. Just ice activity."

"You think he ice picked?"

"Yes, sir, possibly. But whatever he did, we've lost our element of surprise. It's a level playing field right now. I recommend disengaging and waiting it out."

"He's a sitting duck now," Brody said.

"He's alerted," Parks said.

"We know his location. We can fire torpedoes and auto-detonate them. If we don't sink him we'll at least shake him loose."

"We may be off on his location," Parks said. "Plus he'll hear our torpedoes. They'd work like tracer bullets going the wrong way."

Brody leaned forward.

"What's wrong, Pete?"

"Don't mistake me for a coward, sir, but I won't support a suicidal one-for-one exchange."

"The last time we had this conversation, you were afraid I'd gone soft. Now you say you won't support me?"

"This ship has one hundred and twenty-five men relying on you to get them home safe. I think you're pissed that he shot at us and then got away. I think you've turned one-eighty and are out on a vendetta."

Brody looked around the control room. Nobody stood within earshot of his exchange with Parks, but his men seemed to understand the discussion. For the first time since taking the *Miami* against the *Severodvinsk*, he read doubt in his crewmen's faces.

He would have to rebuild their trust.

"Very well," Brody said. "We'll race ahead and ambush him on the other side."

CHAPTER TWENTY-SIX

JUNE 5, 2006
NORTH OF GREENLAND:

S ILENCE AND DARKNESS MADE THE *Colorado*'s missile compartment
surreal. Dim emergency lighting turned Jake's sneakers into sil-
houettes as he watched his steps alternate between the floor and tilted
equipment cabinets. He used piping and valves as monkey-bars while
balancing against the forty-degree starboard list.

An updraft from the bilge carried the rancid scent of leaking trash
bags over Jake's nose as he stooped through a circular hatch into the
forward compartment.

The ship's list facilitated his climb as he ascended to the control
room. A flashlight startled him.

"Get that out of my face," he said.

Seated on a tilted chair, Renard lowered the light.

"My apologies."

Jake rubbed his eyes.

"Yeah, okay," Jake said, "I can't stay too mad at you. You made a
ballsy call putting us on the roof.

"Scotty, you okay?"

The silhouette seated at the ship's control panel ignored Jake. McKenzie's hands trembled in the darkness as they caressed gauges and dials.

"He's not taking it well," Renard said.

"Neither am I, really. I'm not sure what to think. I thought we were home free."

"Maintain your focus. We will work our way through this."

"We just survived a hostile torpedo shot, and our reactor's cooling to cold iron," Jake said.

"Keep your wits about you. You have a crew to lead."

"Where are all the frogmen?"

"In their racks, I pray. Otherwise they're liable to hurt themselves in this abysmal darkness."

"They're big boys and we told them what not to touch," Jake said. "I say we deal with them after we get this pig under control."

"What of affairs aft?" Renard asked. "Ensuring reactor plant integrity is our primary concern. Without our reactor, we're dead."

"There's a lot of lube oil spilling. Bass and Gant are trying to plug the leaks. It's going to be messy, but we can contain them when we start up again."

"And when, *mon ami*, do you forecast that might be? Freezing to death will not be pleasant."

"If we start up now, we could get shot at again."

"Agreed," Renard said. "The noise would be an unacceptable risk. We will have to rely upon the battery."

"If we drain it, we won't have enough juice to get the plant started," Jake said.

"Can't we just pull control rods to heat up the reactor whenever we want?" McKenzie asked.

Jake hadn't expected words from McKenzie. He studied the mechanic. Hollow eyes stared back at him.

"That won't work," Jake said. "It's complex. You need coolant flow and coolant pumps. We need battery power to start up again."

"What about natural circulation?" McKenzie asked.

"Only works if we can remove heat. We need the steam cycle going full swing to do that, and that means steam plant pumps."

"I hear freezing to death is peaceful," McKenzie said.

"We're not going to...shut up!"

McKenzie turned back to his panel. His shaking hands fiddled with de-energized dials and gauges.

"We should consider bringing the sonar room back online, too," Renard said. "We should determine if we're alone yet."

"Starting a motor-generator set is too noisy. We're stuck without AC power."

Renard drew a Marlboro from his crumpled pack.

"I suppose you're correct," Renard said.

"You should take that cigarette out of your mouth. We can't filter the smoke anymore."

"Ah, I'd forgotten."

Renard stuck the cigarette back in its pack.

"I think we can insulate a few staterooms with blankets and make use of body heat," Jake said. "We'll secure space heaters throughout the ship except for a few staterooms."

"That could work, but not indefinitely."

"It'll work as long as it takes to be sure we're alone," Jake said. "A couple days. Maybe longer."

"And what of daily necessities?"

"We'll store canned food and potable water. Each room has a sink we can piss in. For garbage and shit, we'll use freezer bags."

"How I love submarine life," Renard said.

"Scotty," Jake said. "We need to achieve level deck. Can you flood the centerline tank without making noise?"

McKenzie placed his hands in his lap but said nothing.

"Scotty!" Jake said. "Flood the centerline tank until we slip down from the roof."

McKenzie stood and looked at the floor.

"I've got to go operate the valve manually," he said and lumbered down the stairs, leaving Jake with Renard.

"What do you think about our hunter?" Jake asked.

"Someone tried to kill us," Renard said, "and may be close enough to shoot again if we so much as drop a spoon. It's probably your friend from the *Miami*."

"I have a sick feeling it's Brody," Jake said.

"Quite possible, but I'm afraid we may not have the time we need to wait in silence. There are six commandos onboard who feel a sense of urgency."

"Then you'd better tell them that we're going to spend a few days in the dark."

★

The Chief of Naval Operations felt his guts twist as he entered the Oval Office. President Ryder looked up, and Mesher read tension in his face.

"I understand that we've lost contact with the *Miami*, Admiral? This better not be another submarine catastrophe."

"We shouldn't assume that the *Miami* is under duress. There's no evidence. It's probably still under the ice and unable to make radio transmission."

"This country cannot tolerate another American submarine being lost at sea. You'd better be right."

"Sir, I do have some concern with the nature of the *Miami*'s mission."

"The nature?"

"One of my admirals assigned the *Miami* to follow its captain's hunch that the *Colorado* was still alive and heading under the ice."

"I thought we had proof that the *Colorado* sank? We have tapes from over a dozen sonar systems examined by an army of PhD's. What the hell did they say?"

"The acoustic lab at Hopkins is working around the clock. It's laborious work."

"They must know something by now!"

"We know that the weapon that sank the *Colorado* was not an American torpedo," Mesher said.

Ryder stood and paced.

"You're telling me that a random assailant broke through our perimeter undetected, found one of the quietest submarines on the planet, sank it, and got away unnoticed?"

Mesher sensed the impending doom of a shameful end to an illustrious career.

"We won't know until the lab dissects this further or until the underwater search team finds the wreckage on the bottom of the Atlantic."

"You don't seem to know much about your submarines, Admiral."

"These are demanding tasks that require time."

Ryder stood and stared out the window.

"I assume that you at least know where to find the door."

★

Renard shut the door to the executive officer's stateroom. He shivered under his parka.

"*Merde de l'eau!* It's freezing out there."

"I feel the draft," McKenzie said.

Renard noted that McKenzie appeared to have regained his wits.

Layers of bedspreads muffled Renard's steps as he passed through a polished metal bathroom into the commanding officer's quarters.

Covered by comforters, Bass and Gant were sleeping on mattresses atop blankets spread over the floor. Wearing a parka, Jake sprawled out in the commanding officer's fold-out wall rack.

"What's up?" Jake asked.

"This ship's an iceberg," Renard said.

"Battery's still okay?"

"It's only lost three volts over two days."

"We can do this for a few more days, then."

"The other half of our crew is growing impatient."

"They haven't complained."

"You've only talked to Mister Lion. The younger ones do not share his patience. It might be wise to consider the reactor start-up now."

"That's too risky, and you know it," Jake said.

Bass and Gant stirred, and Jake lowered his voice.

"The *Miami* shot at us and missed," Jake said, "and Brody didn't hear us evade. There's a good chance he's still out there."

"You're right, of course," Renard said.

"Then what's the problem?"

"The Taiwanese do not understand why we wait now and why we were moving so slowly under the ice. They think that a steel ship would just bounce off ice ridges unscathed."

"Then they're idiots."

"They do not understand the dangers of this world that you and I take for granted."

"So what should I do?"

"You have a battery at ninety-two percent charge. That's more than adequate for a reactor start-up, right?"

"Yeah."

"Let's risk starting a motor generator and bringing up the sonar room. If we hear nothing, then we start the reactor. If we hear something, then the Taiwanese will have to accept more freezing days. And sadly, so will I."

★

Lieutenant Commander Lin wiped gravy from his lips and looked up at the *Tai Chiang's* wardroom seats. Three men surrounding him ate in silence.

"Pass the salt," he said.

Lieutenant Yang Kai-huang, his executive officer, plopped the shaker by Lin's hand. Yang's face remained glacial. Lin's past attempts at conversation about financial markets had stymied the machinist's son, and lighthearted chat in the wardroom had tapered to nothing.

I dine with the son of a commoner, Lin thought. *How can a man raised in simplicity master the complex art of war? He should be tilling the land.*

A phone chimed by Lin's side. He reached to the wall and lifted the receiver to his ear. He heard news that excited him and pushed the receiver into its cradle.

He stood.

"Come, Yang," he said. "If you pay keen attention, you may learn something."

★

Lin climbed a ladder and slid his soft stomach over one of the many spare barrels of jet fuel he had picked up in a southern Japanese port. Entering the bridge, he studied a young bridge officer.

"Report, Ensign," he said.

"Sir, undersea laser detection bearing three-zero-five. Range four miles. Depth one hundred feet."

"Warm up torpedoes," Lin said.

"Sir, I've turned away from the contact to open distance," the ensign said.

"That is a mistake," Lin said. "The contact is close enough to detect us. We must assume counter-detection and prosecute."

The ensign lowered his gaze.

"Sir, the submarine shows no evidence that it sees or hears us," Yang said. "Our orders are to remain undetected."

"You will report to the auxiliary bridge for battle stations, Mister Yang."

"Sir, our orders state that we are to avoid all encounters unless we have clear evidence that we've been counter-detected."

"I have interpreted that a submerged contact at short range is a threat to our stealth. You will be relieved of your duties and restricted to your quarters for insubordination if you do not follow my orders."

Yang retraced his steps down the stairs. Lin sat at his battle control station.

"This is the captain," he said. "The submerged contact is emanating the frequencies of a *Romeo* class diesel submarine. The ship is Chinese and is a threat."

Through his earpiece, he heard Yang protest.

"The ship shows no indication that it has detected us. We should evade or we risk revealing our position, and that is against our orders," Yang said.

"You are relieved," Lin said. "Lieutenant Second Class Ye, lay below and relieve Lieutenant Yang of auxiliary bridge command."

Over the circuit, Lin heard Yang's headphones slam against his battle control station keyboard.

"Extending torpedo batteries...solution set...firing tube one!" Lin said. "Firing tube two! Weapons away. Coming to course zero-three-five to evade."

Lin listened to his weapons converging on the diesel submarine. He savored the sound of the rupturing hull and turned the *Tai Chiang* northward.

★

Standing in the *Colorado*'s sonar room, Renard slapped his gloves together. Jake's teeth chattered by his ear.

"Shit, Pierre. I've never been this cold," Jake said.

"Be thankful we have space heaters. Otherwise, we would have already frozen to death."

Renard watched Jake flip switches. Machines whirred to life and green displays energized.

"So far, Jake, I see nothing. This is good."

"Give the integrators time to process. Plus our towed array sonar is dangling below us. I don't know how bad that screws up the bearings."

"We're not worried about bearings. Either the arrays hear something or they do not. I pray for the latter case."

After half an hour of space heater operation, Renard still saw his breath but could feel his extremities.

"I think we're alone, Jake. Whoever shot at us may have left."

"I agree. Let's start up this pig and get moving."

★

During the days guiding the *Miami* by the pole toward the Bering Strait, Brody tried seven times to break through the ice but failed. On his eighth try, he watched the depth gauge stall at seventy-five feet.

"Our under-ice sonar predicted that this was the thinnest ice we've seen, right, executive officer?" he asked.

"Yes, sir. Must be a slow thaw."

"We're south of the Alaskan Pipeline, and we still can't get through. I think it's time to just clear the ice altogether."

CHAPTER TWENTY-SEVEN

IS TRICEPS MUSCLES BULGING THROUGH parka sleeves, Tiger finished his hundredth push-up on the stateroom's blanketed floor. His breath formed mist as he spoke in Mandarin to Jaguar in the rack above.

"You wait until I'm done," Tiger said. "Then you can have the floor for your exercises. Or you can go to the engine room. The heaters are on there."

"I will wait," Jaguar said. "I do not want to freeze to death walking back there. I wish we were off of this submarine. The stupid American naval officer has added days to this mission for nothing."

The room's third commando, the wiry Cheetah, responded from the highest rack.

"Slate is starting the reactor now," Cheetah said. "Why are you complaining? He has kept you alive, has he not?"

Tiger felt like slapping Cheetah for being complacent, but he let the two above him argue while he pumped out push-ups.

"He performed so well that we were hunted under the ice," Jaguar said.

"He avoided the torpedo," Cheetah said.

"The Frenchman saved us. Not the American," Jaguar said.

"Slate shut us down to fool the torpedo."

"All he did was shut off the heat so that we had to spend two days in this small room. Then when he listened on sonar, there was no one near us. We wasted two days freezing."

"He did not waste our time," Cheetah said. "He made a tactical decision. You do not stand watch with him. I do. He knows this ship and how to command it."

"I could say the same of the Frenchman," Jaguar said. "When I see how quickly he figures out things on this submarine, it does not seem so impressive. The country needs the warheads, not our caution. Slate is taking his time for no good reason."

As Tiger finished his hundred and twentieth push-up, he heard Cheetah call upon him.

"What do you say, Shin?"

Tiger stood, shook his arms, and pointed at Cheetah's nose.

"I'm telling Sergeant Kao to inform the American that we need to drive faster than five knots."

"What if he disagrees?" Cheetah asked and pushed Tiger's finger away.

"Then I will put a steak knife into Slate's heart myself. This slow speed is cowardice."

★

In maneuvering, Jake flipped switches on the reactor panel and heard concern in Renard's voice.

"The plant is completely liquid?" Renard asked.

"Yeah. Solid plant. The steam pocket in the pressurizer vessel condensed. I've got the pressurizer heaters on, and I'm starting a pair of coolant pumps to heat us up with flow friction," Jake said.

"The lack of a compressed vapor bubble in the primary piping makes pressure control complex, is that not right?"

"Yes. Bass is on the phone with Gant in middle level. Gant's going to discharge water into retention tanks if we need to keep pressure down," Jake said.

"How are we doing on pressure, Bass?" Jake asked.

"We're way low," Bass said. "We might not have to discharge."

"Alright," Jake said. "I'm going to start pulling rods. We'll go critical to accelerate the heat up."

Jake twisted a shim switch on the reactor panel. Relays clicked and motors whirred. His gaze flickered across analog digits that rolled off inches of control rod depth within the core.

"How do you know when you're critical?" Renard asked.

"You forgot?"

"It has something to do with neutron count acceleration."

"Bingo."

Jake nodded at the neutron count meter.

"We're still way sub-critical, but you can see the neutron population just beginning to accelerate."

Minutes passed. Jake released the shim switch. Motors droned and stopped.

"Neutron count is trying to hold," he said. "Baby wants to go critical a half inch below critical rod height...nope, not quite."

"May I smoke now?" Renard asked.

"Just because we're nearing criticality?"

"No, because I'm dying for a cigarette."

"Sure, and...the reactor is critical," Jake said. "I'll keep withdrawing rods into the functional range."

He felt a tickle in his throat and coughed.

"Sorry," Renard said and lowered his cigarette.

"Can't you do something useful?" Jake asked.

"Yes, of course. How can I help?"

"Go read the gyroscopic navigators reset procedure. That's next on our list. It'll take fifteen hours to reset them."

"Fifteen hours?"

"You'd risk under-ice travel without inertial navigation?"

"Of course not," Renard said. "It would be suicide."

"The full procedure for resetting the gyroscopic navigators takes three weeks tied to a pier. I'm doing the condensed version while drifting under an icecap. We'll be lucky if we know our location within five miles."

"Then I suppose it will dismay you to hear that Mister Lion recently informed me that his team is very concerned about the five knot speed limitation you've imposed."

"How concerned?" Jake asked.

"Enough to make me worry."

★

John Brody dreamt of his wife Carole. His subconscious mind relived his honeymoon. She wore a red satin backless dress that caressed her soft brown skin on a moonlit Jamaican beach.

Carole slipped away. A new image wearing a bathrobe appeared, fifteen pounds heavier, with a scornful expression. Cold eyes locked with him as she said that she was leaving.

The dream disappeared as a fist hammered Brody's door.

"Messenger, sir. The Officer of the Deck requests your presence in the control room."

Brody squinted at a digital display that showed eight knots - seven knots slower than he had prescribed. He slipped into his jump suit and trotted to the control room.

Jerry Skiff, the *Miami*'s navigation officer, furrowed his brow.

"Sir, under-ice sonar indicated that the roof was starting to slant down on us. I went deeper, but we're getting squeezed to the floor. I wanted you here before I went any further."

Brody rubbed his eyes. His sleep had been fitful.

"Are we on track?" he asked.

"Yes, sir," Skiff said. "I've double-checked three times. We're in the deepest water around here and should have cleared the ice by now, but we're hitting a dead end."

"The charted paths are no guarantee for what Mother Nature does with the ice year to year," Brody said. "We're lucky we made it this far without having to turn around. Slow to four knots, push until we get thirty feet above and below us, and then turn east. There's got to be a way around this ridge."

★

Jake sat in the captain's chair in the *Colorado*'s wardroom. He suppressed a cough as Renard indulged in a drag of his Marlboro. Commandos filled six of the remaining eight chairs with Kao by his side.

"Mister Slate, we are concerned that five knots speed will cost us too much time," Kao said. "We are already nine days behind schedule. The rendezvous ship may not wait."

"I planned for up to two weeks of contingencies. That's how long the rendezvous ship should be willing to wait for us," Jake said.

For the first time, Jake saw the younger men protest. He could not understand their Mandarin, but he heard its biting tone. Kao snapped a word and they fell silent.

"Every day is added risk for the rendezvous ship, and for the nation itself," Kao said. "They need the warheads now."

"Look, we have a ripped right fairwater plane from the aircraft attack, and we probably just bent the left one against the roof. That means noise, and there's probably someone still looking for us."

"Moving slow did not prevent us from being hunted once before. Perhaps speed is a superior tactical alternative."

Jake felt reality inverting as a Taiwanese commando told him how to drive a Trident submarine under the ice.

"Safety dictates that we move slowly," he said. "Our navigation is going to be inaccurate due to the gyroscopic navigators restart. We'll have a tough time working through this maze, and we could smack our bow into an ice wall if we go too fast."

Kao directed his question to Renard, and Jake felt his authority slipping.

"You have experience, Mister Renard. What is the real danger if we impact an ice structure?"

"Jake's concerns are well founded," Renard said. "With the complete and alert crew on the *Amethyst*, I would brave fifteen knots. With this sluggish Trident and its personnel limitations, I would fear more than say, eight – and that as an extreme."

"Eight knots. At least you agree that-" Kao said.

"Ten!" Jake said.

The room quieted. Jake stared at Kao.

"Ten knots, Mister Lion. Mister Renard doesn't realize how long our ballast tanks are against those of his precious *Amethyst*. If we go ten knots, I can make up for two days. If something goes wrong and we smack the ice, then we have a sonar dome and three ballast tanks to take the blow. We'll crumple like a car hood, but we might live."

Kao's face remained stone.

"Is this acceptable?" Jake asked.

"Ten knots is acceptable," Kao said.

Jake pushed back his chair and walked out of the room, slamming the door behind him.

★

As he squatted in his shower stall, Jake let hot water pour over his back. He lowered his head into his hands. The heat melted the artic chill from his bones, but the chill in his soul remained ice.

The Frenchman had been right weeks ago when they had intercepted the *Custom Venture*. His few friends were gone, or at best distant. He was empty and alone - living for survival itself.

He wanted to trust Renard. The Frenchman had proven himself a worthy ally thus far, but everything he had done for Jake was self-serving. He wondered if Renard would jab a knife in his back when their agendas crossed.

Jake accepted that he might never be able to trust anyone. He curled into a ball and let the water burn away at an icy core that wouldn't seem to melt.

Renard dreamt...

He sat on a slab of granite atop Mont Saint Victoire. Storm clouds swallowed the mountain. As freezing rain pelted his face, he saw a dark figure pierce the swirling blackness and disappear.

He assumed it a dragon or some other nightmarish beast, but he heard jet engines whine between cracks of lightning.

Stinking of blood and gunpowder, a pistol appeared in his hands. He tightened his grip and rose to his feet.

A puddle of mud chilled his first barefooted step. He froze. A black serpent slithered over his foot and vanished into bushes behind a boulder. Renard followed it around a corner, and two men locked in combat came into view.

Jake wore a charred cotton jump suit and bounced on his feet. Facing him, a middle-aged Taiwanese commando in a black wetsuit approached, his legs spread wide and his rigid hand forward.

Lightning flashed, and Jake unleashed a flurry of kicks. He connected with Kao's ear, and the commando staggered. Lightning cracked again, and Kao buried his heel into Jake's gut.

Mud splashed on Renard's feet as Jake landed before him. The tugging at his pants reminded him of a widow he had long ago created. He wondered if he was ruining another life as Jake clawed at his rain-drenched cotton dress shirt.

"Help me!" Jake said.

"What should I do?" Renard asked.

"You got me into this, you bastard. Get me out!"

Lightning crashed. Renard awoke.

Renard showered away cold sweat. He pulled his shirt over his shoulder and studied his reflection.

His eyes looked dull, and his skin sagged.

His knees cracked as he climbed the stairs to the control room where he joined Jake by the navigation chart and studied the coordinates that placed the *Colorado* one hundred miles north of Alaska.

"Shit, Pierre," Jake said. "You look as tired as I feel."

Renard lit a Marlboro.

"You handled the confrontation well yesterday."

"Are we in this too deep?" Jake asked.

"The dangers within the ship now equal those outside."

"Yeah, even though my friend on the *Miami* is the one who tried to kill us."

"You verified the acoustic evidence from the torpedo exchange?" Renard asked.

"I ran the tape," Jake said.

"Then it is as we feared. The best submarine commander in the world, present company excluded, is on our tail."

Renard inhaled. The sweetness of nicotine filled his lungs and he blew smoke away from Jake.

"And I've got a revolt brewing within the ship," Jake said, "and there's a chance that this submarine might become an 'us versus them' world. Six frogmen against four sailors is normally no match, but remember, this is my ship."

"Stop reminding me."

"Well, it is, and I keep a few tricks up my sleeve. I don't know who the hell you became after commanding the *Amethyst*, and I don't know how deep you're in with the Taiwanese. But if it comes down to it, you'll need to choose a side."

Sadly, he's correct, Renard thought. *The situation on this ship is more volatile than he knows.*

★

Brody ran his finger over a penciled trace of the *Miami's* voyage. From the plot's overhead perspective, he reviewed a path once sealed by ice, a turn to the east, and then a southerly trek under an ice roof that ascended into the Arctic Ocean's southern body of water, the Chukchi Sea.

He walked to the periscope and stuck his eye to the optics as the *Miami* ascended. Daylight broke through the Arctic Ocean and painted shallow water turquoise. Brody swiveled the scope. A wall of white ice rose behind him and an iceberg touched the horizon.

"No close contacts," he said. "Chief of the Watch, raise the radio mast. Radio room, transmit one outgoing message. Let the world know that we found the *Colorado*."

★

In Nome, Alaska, Grant Mercer cast a line off a forty-eight foot trawler.

As he tiptoed his way along the deck with the agility learned while operating his father's sailboat on Lake Michigan, he felt the idling three hundred horsepower diesels rumbling below.

Under the canopy of the powerboat's pilothouse, he nudged an aircraft-type throttle. Mercer watched the bow push aside chunks of ice as he entered the darkness of the Snake River en route to the Chukchi Sea.

CHAPTER TWENTY-EIGHT

JUNE 14, 2006
CHUKCHI SEA, NORTH OF THE BERING STRAIT:

FOUR DAYS HAD PASSED SINCE Brody had led the *Miami* from the icecap. After communicating with higher authorities, he had two P-3 Orion crews from Whidbey Island, Washington, in a dedicated full alert status to back him up. Two submarines from Hawaii, still a day's transit away, were en route to the Bering Strait to assist.

Brody steered the *Miami* back and forth along the ten-mile wide underwater opening that he believed offered the *Colorado* its only passage from under the ice.

His latest orders matched his instincts – destroy Jake Slate and the *Colorado*.

★

As the ice-roof clamped down upon the submarine, the under-ice sonar system blared. Jake reached for a microphone to order Bass to slow the ship, but the deck fell.

He grabbed for a handrail and regained his balance, but his legs hit his chest as the *Colorado* scraped the ocean floor. He felt the ship rebound and graze the overhead ice again.

Silence. Jake hoped the collision was over.

It wasn't.

A handrail knocked the air out of his lungs. He winced as crumpling metal creaked. Splintering ice snapped. The shattering fiberglass bow crackled.

Expecting a wall of water to crash in, Jake held his breath. Chunks of ice banged the *Colorado*. A circular rib in a ballast tank groaned and buckled.

Jake stood and stumbled across the slanted deck.

At the helm, the wiry Cheetah lay limp over the rudder control yoke.

"You okay?" Jake asked.

Cheetah nodded, palpated his stomach, and winced.

Broken ribs, Jake thought.

Jake moved to Kao, who was hunched over the ship's control panel. Blood covered his forehead. Jake cradled Kao and set him on the deck.

Cheetah, bent to his side, limped toward Jake.

"Take care of him," Jake said.

Standing, Jake grabbed a phone and called the engine room. After learning that Mike Gant had escaped harm but that Leopard had broken his arm, he saw Renard appear atop the staircase.

"What happened?" Renard asked.

"Ice ridge came out of nowhere. Mister Lion's hurt pretty bad. Mister Cheetah's probably got some busted ribs. Gant's fine, but Mister Leopard's got a broken arm."

"I banged against the side of my rack," Renard said, "but no major damage. I think most of us who were sleeping are okay. How's the ship?"

"We're on the bottom, but I don't know much else."

"Look at our under-ice sonar," Renard said. "I no longer think we're stuck."

"What?"

"The roof. It's sixty feet above."

"That correlates to charted water depth," Jake said.

Jake watched a sardonic smile form on Renard's face.

"Your methods are most brutal, but I must congratulate you on clearing the icepack."

★

Brody scurried to the *Miami*'s control room.

"Captain, the sonar room called it an ice event, but now they think it's sounding like the *Colorado*," Parks said.

"What do you have?"

"Cracking noise, and lots of it, but afterwards we picked up metallic crumpling and popping on the same bearing. Something hit the ice hard."

"Do you think the *Colorado* hit the ridge we cleared four days ago?"

"That's my guess, sir."

Brody envisioned the impact of a Trident smacking ice. The sonar dome would be damaged, and the warped metal of the bow would add flow noise to an already battle-scarred submarine. He had found his prey, and it was wounded.

"If the *Colorado* isn't already flooding," Brody said, "we'll close in and finish her off."

★

Jake entered the missile compartment and coughed out toxic fumes. He reached for a cubby with stenciled red 'E-A-B' letters, grabbed a canvas bag, and pulled out a facemask.

With the rush of air and a snap, he popped his Emergency Air Breather EAB line into a forced air breathing station, pressed the facemask to his cheeks, sucked stale air and tightened straps around his head.

Wisps of black floated by his face mask. Gulping a last breath, he disconnected from the air supply and held his breath, pinched his air line, and descended the ladder to the missile compartment's lowest deck.

Here, he pressed his air line into a copper fitting and exhaled. His lungs burned, and he craved the ensuing breath. Hoping his connection was valid, he sucked from his mask. Clean air filled his lungs.

Above the bilge, a high-pressure air valve fanned a glowing flame. Orange danced against a paste-green lagging canvas.

Jake gulped and disconnected. He walked to an extinguisher and hauled it back to his air connection. Heat billowed over him as he shot smothering foam over the lagging. When the foam stream sputtered and died, he dropped the canister and retraced his steps to the air.

Smoke rose above the green hull insulation. A tiny flame burst through the white foam. Jake took a breath and retreated.

★

His EAB facemask slung over his shoulder, Jake climbed up the ladder to the control room.

"Fire in missile compartment lower level!" he said.

"How bad?" Renard asked.

"I don't know but it's in the hull lagging and getting fanned by a busted air reducer. An extinguisher did no good. We need hoses. Fast."

"I will summon the crew," Renard said.

The entire eleven-man crew - sans Gant and Leopard stranded a world away in the engine room on the fire's far side - assembled around Jake.

For the first time, Jake noted the commandos looking more spooked than the sailors. His men were trained for damage control, but fire in an inescapable confined space was a new horror to the frogmen.

"We've got a hull lagging fire in missile compartment lower level," Jake said. "We'll use two hoses to keep the fire from spreading aft while we push it forward and douse it. We're going to use EAB's on a buddy system."

"Bass," Jake said, "take Mister Tiger and hook his air line into yours on a buddy-breathe. Flake out hose nine on the third level and attack from above. I'll take Mister Panther and get it done at the source with hose twelve. Grab some EAB's and wait for me at the third level watertight door. Scott, take Mister Jaguar to the oxygen breathing apparatus locker, put on the OBA's, and get into fire fighting suits. We might need you guys on self-contained air. When you're geared up, join us with hose ten. Go."

Men scrambled. Jake turned to Renard.

"Get us off the bottom to level the deck so we can fight this thing."

Jake studied Kao, who leaned his head into paper towels held by the wincing Cheetah. Blood trickled from a forehead gash, and indigo and black discoloration covered his eye. His fingers trembled, and Jake expected that the commando was entering shock and would pass out.

He slipped by the injured commandos and flipped knobs that directed pressure from trim tanks to the fire main.

"There's a first aid kit in the galley when you have time," he said and descended the stairs.

Jake met his firefighting team and peered through the tiny window into the missile compartment. Thick smoke filled the other side.

"Mister Panther, I'm going to hook into this air manifold. Once I do, hook your EAB into the manifold on my belt. Then slip your mask on."

Jake tasted stale air. He heard his muffled voice resonate from his EAB mouthpiece.

"Can you hear me?"

Panther nodded.

"Good, because you won't see me when we're in there. Whatever you do, don't panic or we're dead. I can find any manifold in that compartment. Just inhale when I tell you and keep an arm on me while we're moving. Got it?"

"Yes," the wide-eyed commando said.

"Ready, inhale!" Jake said.

He tugged open the circular door to the missile compartment and stepped into dark smoke. Moving through opaqueness, he groped for a ladder, pinched his air hose between his fingers, grabbed the railing, and stepped down the rungs. The commando's sneakers bumped his head on the way down.

When he reached the deck, Jake's lungs were burning. He felt the commando's weight hit the deck and his hand slap his shoulder. Jake grabbed the hand, moved to the nearest air manifold, and clicked his hose.

"Inhale!" Jake said.

Jake sucked several breaths while sweat trickled from his brow. Crackling flames started to roar.

"Around the corner. Ready?" he asked.

"Ready!" Panther said.

"Inhale!"

Jake reached the coil of hose twelve and drew breaths from a nearby manifold. He heaved the hose's bronze and plastic nozzle to the deck.

Tossing lengths about the floor, he unraveled the hose, giving it room to expand. He twisted a valve and watched the hose bulge with water pressure.

"Can you reach the nozzle?" Jake asked.

"I have it," Panther said. "There is no water pressure."

Jake grabbed the hose, jerked, and straightened a kink. He returned the nozzle to Panther.

"Drag this. We're moving aft. Ready, inhale."

Jake reached a manifold, clicked the air line, and breathed.

"Stand behind me. Press down," he said.

Jake pointed the nozzle at the flames and flipped forward a piece of bronze. His chest and arms tensed against the backlash. He welcomed Panther's weight over the hose.

A conical burst of water shot at the hull lagging. From above, sheets of water from Bass' hose cascaded down the curved hull. Squinting at the flame, Jake watched the fire outpace the efforts of two hoses.

Clouds of black enveloped him. The fire spread into the bilges and created a wall of flames that blocked Jake's forward escape route. He shut and dropped the nozzle.

"It's over! Forget it. Let's go. Engine room. Ready, inhale!"

When they reached the back of the missile compartment, Jake could again see his companion's opaque shape. He shouted to Panther to inhale, unhooked from the manifold, and started up the ladder to the third level. Reaching the ladder's midpoint, he felt a tug at his belt.

Jake twisted and watched Panther's eyes bulge as he swallowed the vacuum of his facemask. Falling backward, the commando reached for Jake and grabbed his air cord. Jake's mask chafed his cheeks and slid across his face. Smoke burned his eyes.

Jake heard a thump and saw Panther cough, gag, and rip off his facemask. He jumped to the deck and reached, but the commando kicked his arm. He reached again, but his fingers slipped off a flailing arm. His lungs burned, and he craved air.

I need the self-contained air of an OBA to save this guy, he thought.

He popped free from the buddy fitting and left the commando's useless EAB next to its dying owner.

Jake retreated to an air manifold. He plugged in and breathed, but toxins made him want to tear out his lungs. He pried open the seal of his mask and coughed. As he inhaled again, the air tasted less noxious. He expelled air through his mask one more time, unplugged from the manifold, and sought the ladder.

After breathing tainted air in his mask at successive manifolds, Jake saw light through the round window of the engine room's water-tight door. He slapped his hand against the handle, depressed it, and pulled. The door opened and he staggered through.

Ripping off his mask, he knelt and rested his chest on the door-frame's machined ring, inhaling deep, rapid breaths. Then he stood, held his breath in the path of the flowing smoke, and shut the door behind him. In the narrow tunnel through the reactor compartment, he fell to all fours and shut his eyes while he cried to clean the smoke from them.

When he opened his eyes, he saw Tiger, a mountain of muscle, towering over him. The broad-shouldered commando screamed.

"Where is Chanlin?"

Chanlin, Jake thought. *Mister Panther has a real name.*

"I said where is Chanlin!"

Jake looked up at Tiger's smoke-covered cheeks. Black pupils seemed to pop from the husky commando's head.

"You left him to die."

"He panicked. I had to leave him, but I can save him. There's a mobile OBA breathing system at the engine room damage control locker. I can put it on in thirty seconds and have him back in here in ninety seconds. We can revive him."

The commando stepped aside.

CHAPTER TWENTY-NINE

"Captain, their engine room is still up, but there's no flow noise, no screw noise, no blade noise. The *Colorado*'s not going anywhere," Schmidt said.

"We've closed twenty miles, and they're still sixty miles off," Brody said.

"They're farther than I thought."

"They hit hard, didn't they?"

"Real hard, sir."

Brody entered the *Miami*'s control room and tapped Pete Parks on the shoulder. Parks' brown eyes appeared glassy as he analyzed the data on the *Colorado*.

"Executive officer, join me over the navigation plot," Brody said.

Brody leaned over a bird's eye view of the icecap.

A convex arc outlined the ice wall separating the Arctic Ocean from the Chukchi Sea. An 'X' had been stenciled where lines of noise from the *Miami*'s zigzag path converged on the resting place of the *Colorado*. He walked a pair of dividers across the paper.

"Sixty-one miles to the *Colorado*. I still can't believe how far sound carries under the ice," he said.

"Makes our job easier, sir," Parks said.

"Easier, yes. Easy, no. Remember the last time we shot at this guy?"

"Yes, sir. And now he's bottomed, which will make the shot just as hard for our torpedo as last time."

"But he won't have a chance to shut down his plant again if he doesn't hear the weapon."

"The high-speed screws will be audible if his sonar system still works."

"I'll shoot a slow speed shot so he won't hear it," Brody said.

"The active seeker will tip him off."

"Not if I shoot a passive shot. The torpedo can swim up to him and he'll never hear it."

"I concur sir, but we'll need to get close and perfect our targeting data. We've got to be gnat's ass dead on."

"Pete, he used to be my friend, but he's toyed with me across two oceans. When I tell the Commodore how I finally put an end to this, I'm going to tell him I did it right. I don't care how close I have to get, I'm shoving an ADCAP torpedo up the *Colorado's* tailpipe."

★

From one maneuvering doorway to the other, Tiger barked at Leopard. Tiger and his comrade had Gant and Bass pinned in the engine room's control center.

"He left Chanlin to die," Tiger said in Mandarin. "He's trying to revive him, but what of it? We don't need the Americans. I say we kill them now!"

"We're two against three in the engine room, and my arm is broken. Kao also warned us that Slate is trained in martial arts," Leopard said.

"I will kill them all myself," Tiger said, savoring the worry in Bass and Gant's faces. He reached into the tiny control room for a microphone and yelled in a language that was unbreakable code to the westerners.

"Kao, Slate left Chanlin to die in the missile compartment. Let me kill them!"

"Mister Tiger sounds upset." Renard said.

"The fire grew out of control, and Mister Panther was an unfortunate casualty," Kao said.

"I'm sorry for the loss," Renard said.

Jaguar caught Renard's eye as he climbed the stairs to the control room and darted to Kao to relieve the injured Cheetah from holding a washcloth over his leader's left eye. McKenzie, pulling his facemask over his head, followed Jaguar. Black flex hoses suspended the mask behind his back.

"The fire's out of control," McKenzie said. "No way we can fight it. We're going to have to let it burn itself out."

A dead commando...a fire between Slate and me, Renard thought. *A potential war...neutrality may be impossible.*

Renard watched as Jaguar discarded blood-soaked towels into a waste bin and helped Kao stand. Kao reached into the overhead but staggered. Jaguar stabilized his commander and handed him the microphone.

"Mister Tiger, we mourn the loss of our comrade," Kao said. "We will pay honor to him upon our return home."

He switched to Mandarin. Renard decoded no words but intuited the meaning. Kao had ordered Tiger to kill the Americans.

★

"Do you have a knife?" Tiger asked in Mandarin.

"A small blade," Leopard said.

Tiger twisted his neck to see Jake running behind him toward the missile compartment.

"We will deal with Slate later," he said. "But I will begin by killing Bass."

Tiger launched a side-kick that hyper-extended Bass' knee, and he buckled against the electric panel. Then the commando stabbed his index finger knuckle through Bass' windpipe. Bass clutched his throat, and his face turned red. Tiger heard the American's face slap linoleum and stepped on Bass' back as he convulsed, suffocated, and died.

Leopard jabbed the knife into Gant's lung, followed him as he fell to the deck and dropped a knee into his back. He pushed Gant's head and slid the blade through his carotid artery.

★

Jake breathed from the mask of a self-contained oxygen breathing apparatus. The OBA's oxygen canister and heavy brass fittings bounced against his chest with each stride. He glanced down the tunnel.

A chill raced up his spine as he saw Bass on the floor. Tiger looked up, hollered, and charged.

"You are next, Slate!"

Jake ducked through the watertight door to the missile compartment and started to push the door shut behind him, then reconsidered.

He wiggled between pipes behind the door, held the door latch, and watched smoke race through the portal. Tiger grabbed the door's opposite side and, coughing, battled Jake for control of it, but billowing smoke overcame the commando. The struggle ceased and Jake latched the door open.

He let his breathing slow and watched airborne poisons from the missile compartment rush into the engine room. When he was confident that the engine room had filled with smoke, he returned.

Walking over Bass' body, he entered maneuvering and stared at a pond of blood draining from Gant's neck. To avenge his colleagues, he targeted the two commandos in the engine room as his first victims.

Outside maneuvering, he stopped at an EAB manifold system air reducer. Groping through opaque smoke, he found machined cubes. He ran his hands over the system and shut an inlet valve. To be certain that he had sentenced Tiger and Leopard to death, he closed the outlet valve, too.

After breathing the scant air remaining in the header downstream of the reducer, the two commandos in the engine room would die of either suffocation or smoke inhalation.

Jake turned his thoughts toward the three Taiwanese men in the forward compartment. They would freeze to death within hours if he cut off their electrical power. Although he might be condemning McKenzie to death, he doubted that the machinist mate still lived.

He pushed through billowing clouds into the smoky cavern of the missile compartment and felt his way to one of the ship's firefighting thermal imagers. He knelt by a box, removed its Velcro strap, and withdrew the missile compartment's imager, then placed the thermal video camera against his facemask.

The missile compartment became an eerie light blue. The burning distant forward section of the compartment appeared white. Behind Jake, the open engine room watertight door appeared as a circle of cold navy blue. To his left, twin electrical distribution towers glowed azure.

He knelt between the towers and lowered the imager, then ran his fingers across Plexiglas shields until he found protruding knobs, which he twisted and removed. With the shields by his side and the breakers exposed, he depressed buttons. Springs hammered the breakers open.

Jake grasped the imager and returned to the engine room.

He retrieved spare OBA canisters, dropped them in maneuvering, and slid shut the maneuvering doors. He then reached overhead and rotated a lever. Seven-hundred pound per square inch air whistled into the tiny room.

Feeling his ears pop, he cracked open the starboard door. Air displaced smoke. Jake rolled the door shut again and sat.

He lifted his facemask. Invisible wisps of smoke invaded his lungs. After a fit of coughing, he breathed the pressurized atmosphere within maneuvering.

He calmed himself and grabbed a microphone. Unsure if it were a useless gesture, he broadcast his voice throughout the ship.

★

Sitting at the ship's control panel, Scott McKenzie was terrified. He listened to Renard trying to calm Kao, but it sounded like empty diplomacy.

"We must be patient," the Frenchman said. "They probably have discovered systems in need of immediate attention. If there were a problem, they would have notified us."

Jake's voice rang from the loudspeakers.

"Scotty, they killed Gant and Bass. Get back here if you want to live!"

McKenzie sprang for the staircase.

Jaguar, the only uninjured commando, dove for him.

Grasping hands sent a shiver up McKenzie's spine, but Jaguar's grip slipped off his shoulders.

Cheetah blocked his escape. The injured commando launched a side-kick into McKenzie's OBA breast plate, howled in pain, and fell to the floor clutching his side.

The kick knocked McKenzie's wind out, and his vision blurred as he jumped down the staircase.

Fighting to expand his lungs, McKenzie sprinted for the watertight door. He ran as if in a nightmare - swimming through molasses.

Something snagged his ankle. The floor smacked him in the chin. His jaw ached, and a weight on his ankles climbed up his legs.

Terrified, he kicked, wiggled to the door, and hurled his arm upward to the latch. Heat from the missile compartment pushed the door open. The opening grew wider and a cloud of choking black smoke filled the passageway.

His legs freed, McKenzie climbed to his feet. He saw Jaguar stand and fumble behind his neck for his facemask.

Amateur, McKenzie thought as he ignored the straps, pressed the mask into a seal over his face, and escaped into the blackness of the missile compartment.

Heat burned through the soles of his sneakers as he slipped into the tight space between the missile tubes. He worked the straps of his mask, slipped on flame-retardant gloves, and walked a memorized path toward the engine room. He waved his hands in the blackness, reaching with each step for the phantom commando he feared chased him. Behind the after tubes, he stopped by a circuit phone.

"Jake? You there?" he asked.

"Scotty? You made it! Where are you?"

"Missile compartment third level. Jake, I'm scared."

"Maneuvering's pressurized. Get back here. We'll be okay."

CHAPTER THIRTY

IN THE SHADOWS OF EMERGENCY lighting, Renard took Kao's arm over his shoulder and inched him down the staircase. Doubled over, Cheetah hobbled below. Jaguar, his face covered with soot, arrived and helped support Kao. He exchanged words in Mandarin with Cheetah.

Renard debated his allegiance. The Taiwanese controlled the forward compartment and his ride home, but Jake controlled the ship's power. Trapped by a fire on the Taiwanese side of the battlefield, he decided to side with Kao's men - for the moment.

In the wardroom, Renard lowered Kao into a chair. He sat and watched the Sergeant shiver in the encroaching coldness. Just as he thought that Kao's shallow breathing had stopped, the commando returned from death.

"What threat does Slate pose?" Kao asked, his voice almost a whisper.

Renard felt like a prisoner advising an enemy.

"From the engine room, he controls almost every resource on the ship – electricity, propulsion, air, water, hydraulics."

Kao's hand slipped from his wound. Jaguar returned from the kitchen and pressed a fresh towel against his leader's forehead.

"Slate also carries the only keys to the gun lockers," Renard said.

"Can we open the forward gun locker?" Kao asked.

"We would freeze to death before we could pick that lock. Slate has the advantage."

Kao's eyes had become slits.

"The men standing behind me are trained to kill," Kao said. "They will take Slate down."

★

Jake read terror in McKenzie's eyes as he entered maneuvering, ripped off his OBA facemask, and coughed.

"What the hell's happening, Jake? Bass is dead. You said no one would get hurt."

"Mister Panther freaked out in the missile compartment. I tried to save him but the Taiwanese went nuts. We're at war. I already got back at the two guys who did this to Gant and Bass. I checked. They're dead."

"What do we do?"

"I already cut their power. We just wait now."

McKenzie sat at a console and ran his finger over an electric motor's control knob.

"Hey, the plant manual says you're not allowed to touch that. You're a mechanic."

McKenzie laughed. It was nervous laughter but it calmed him

"Don't worry, Scotty," Jake said. "We're in control."

★

"I will speak to Slate while your men approach – distract him," Renard said.

He dialed a sound-powered circuit and heard Jake's startled voice.

"Yeah?" Jake asked.

"Pierre here, the friend you once knew before you went insane," Renard said.

"You were never a friend, and you know I'm sane."

"My mistake. I must have taken our friendship for granted. Since you're alive, I will assume that you've killed three men."

"Damn it, Pierre, Mister Panther freaked out. The guy just lost it. I barely saved myself trying to help him. Then his buddies went nuts and killed my guys. What did you expect me to do?"

"So it's two of you against four of us?"

"If you've chosen to play on the losing team. You cold yet?"

Renard studied Kao, who looked unconscious. He then spoke in basic French.

"I'm with you, mon ami. Two men are hunting you with knives. They left thirty seconds ago."

"I was hoping you would make the right choice," Jake said, *"mon ami."*

Jake slammed the phone into its cradle.

"Scotty, change of plans. Put on your OBA. Renard's with us. He says there's two commandos coming with knives."

"What do we do?"

"Shift to new oxygen canisters and get weapons from the aft small arms locker. We'll ambush them in the missile compartment."

"It's pitch black in there," McKenzie said.

"That's the point. They'll be blind and moving slow, but we'll have the imager. We'll wait under the missile compartment hatches. You get a shotgun, and I'll take a pistol. When they get close, I'll guide your shotgun and tap you. Then you pump out rounds. You'll be too close to miss."

"What if they have one of the other imagers?"

"Did you ever tell them about our imagers?"

"No."

"Neither did I."

★

Standing between electric towers in the missile compartment, Jake held the imager to his face. He felt a nine-millimeter pistol under his sneaker, and beside him McKenzie knelt with a shotgun.

Panning the imager, Jake studied the port corridor through the missile compartment upper level. Then the starboard corridor, then down the ladder to the deck below.

Each time he panned the approaches, he expected to see the image of a commando hurling a knife at his heart. He swallowed.

From the deck below, a bluish-white figure groped for a staircase handrail. Bright white, caused by the exothermic reaction of the commando's oxygen breathing canister, burned in the figure's belly. A smaller second figure limped behind the first. Long blades, extensions of cold cobalt through the imager, rose from each man's hand.

Jake held his breath as the men ascended. Reaching for the barrel of McKenzie's shotgun, the white form of his hand extended in front of his imager. He pointed the barrel at the top of the stairs and waited while McKenzie steadied the gun.

★

Renard studied the dying commando.

"Sergeant Kao?" he asked.

Kao peered through caked blood.

"Renard, when you spoke French to Slate, you were hiding something."

Renard feared that Cheetah and Jaguar would kill him if they defeated Jake and learned that he had betrayed them. He feigned allegiance.

"I'm sure your defense minister assured you of my loyalty. My God, I took a bullet through my back trying to help your nation."

Kao grabbed Renard's arm with a strength impossible for a dying man.

"I do not care which side you have chosen," Kao said. "No matter who wins this battle, you will survive. I have ordered my men to spare you. It is you who must see that the warheads are delivered."

★

Through the imager, Jake double-checked McKenzie's shotgun. It pointed at the burning white image of Jaguar's chest plate. He lowered the imager to his feet, grabbed his pistol, and tapped McKenzie three times on the back.

McKenzie's shotgun exploded, clicked, and exploded again as the mechanic pumped the reload chamber and fired. Six shots rang out. The confined echoes hurt Jake's ears.

Jake reached for his imager and studied the carnage. He grabbed his pistol but didn't need it. McKenzie had gutted Jaguar through his chest plate. Cheetah had no head, and the heat rising from the blood spurting from his neck made a milky white pool on the cold steel deck plates.

Jake led McKenzie back to maneuvering's pressurized atmosphere, removed his facemask and grabbed the microphone.

"Gentlemen, there are two of you left. You'll both die if you resist. Contact me in maneuvering to discuss your surrender."

"It's over," Renard said, "Kao is either unconscious or dead. For his sake, I pray it's the latter."

CHAPTER THIRTY-ONE

WITH THE FUEL AND OXYGEN spent, the fire had died, and Jake walked through the ring of ashes that had once been the missile compartment's lagging insulation. He lowered the imager and entered the forward compartment with a nine-millimeter pistol in hand.

Alone, he closed the watertight door, removed his facemask, and unhooked the OBA system. He let it fall from his chest to the ground and rubbed sweat from his face.

Following his pistol barrel, he crept toward the wardroom and stopped at the door.

Let's try a little test, he thought.

He removed the clip from his nine-millimeter and popped bullets one by one into his pocket. He slammed the empty clip back into the weapon and pushed open the door.

His face glistening with perspiration, Renard sat in the captain's chair. He flicked open his gold-plated Zippo lighter under a fresh Marlboro.

"And what now, Jake?"

"We need to get this ship up and running again."

"What about him?"

Kao's wound had swollen his eye shut. Blood caked the lid and dripped into the puddle in which his face lay. Jake felt a weak pulse at Kao's neck and plopped the empty pistol before Renard. The Frenchman lifted it and seemed to measure its weight.

"He's still alive," Jake said. "Do him a favor."

"I will not," Renard said and returned the pistol.

Jake pulled back the slide, retrieved a bullet from his pocket, and dropped it in the chamber. He let the spring slam the slide forward.

"It was unloaded? You bastard!" Renard said.

"Needed to be sure you wouldn't use it on me."

The Frenchman's face flushed. He stood and trembled.

"You've been loathe to consider me an ally since the moment we met. I've protected you, I've guided you, I've trusted you, and I've freed you! When will you stop testing me?"

"I'm satisfied now. I trust you."

"Yes? No more strip searches, no more threats, no more tricks to test me?"

Jake extended his hand.

Renard blew smoke.

"Perhaps you should consider that my patience has worn thin awaiting your trust," Renard said. "I will not tolerate any more doubt."

"Fine."

Renard accepted Jake's hand.

"Good then," Renard said.

The Frenchman inhaled from his cigarette and blew several puffs. The flush fell from his cheeks.

"Well, go ahead, *mon ami*," Renard said.

Jake pressed the barrel against Kao's head. He curled his finger inward but hesitated.

"Or you could let nature take its course," Renard said.

"I don't want any loose ends," Jake said.

Stirring, Kao whispered two words - "Leave me."

"What?" Jake asked.

"Leave me with the weapon and one bullet."

Jake looked at Renard who nodded. He left the pistol on the table and followed Renard out the door.

His heart skipped a beat as a shot rang.

★

Thirty miles from Russian waters, Grant Mercer read a Stephen King novel under a kerosene lamp. Black tape over the trawler's windows trapped light. A kerosene space heater protected him from the freezing cold. He lay the book down, checked the GPS, and deduced that he had drifted ten miles since his last reading.

He braved the cold of the pilot house and depressed a button. Twin diesel engines belched and groaned. Mercer drove the ship ten miles west to the coordinates where Jake had told him to wait. He cut the engines, returned to the cabin, and picked up his novel.

★

The *Tai Chiang* floated near an iceberg and used its short-range blue-green undersea laser system to search for the *Colorado*. The laser detected nothing. Neither did the infrared sweeps. But the ship's sonar system did.

Wearing a thick navy blue sweater, a Taiwanese ensign tapped at his battle control station and reviewed the frequency data from Mercer's diesel engine, but Lin had made it clear that the *Tai Chiang* would not waste precious fuel investigating fishing vessels.

★

Jake watched the ship's control panel. Perceptible only on the control panel's gauges, the Trident ascended. Smashed ballast tanks moaned as the ship settled five feet above the bottom.

Jake spoke via the circuit to McKenzie in the engine room.

"Scott, give the throttles a quarter twist counterclockwise."

The *Colorado* crawled through the hole it had punched in the ice, but Jake heard the ship grind to a stop.

"I think we're riding over our damaged bow," Renard said.

"Agreed. What if we just blow to the surface?"

"The entire hemisphere will know we're here," Renard said.

"May as well send invitations to the party."

Jake pushed handles upward. Air hissed from high-pressure canisters into the ballast tanks on either end of the ship. Jake felt his stomach drop through his knees as the *Colorado* ascended.

He raised a periscope and examined dark water and the crisp white ice behind him. Violent spray shot upward where the forward-most ballast tanks had been smashed and ripped open.

"We're alone, Pierre. How fast are we going?"

"Six knots," Renard said. "I recommend we speed up to reach our rendezvous with the *Tai Chiang*."

"How far are we from the rendezvous point?"

"The gyroscopic navigators are off after the collision, but their last charted fix places us eight miles west and thirty miles north. I will get a GPS fix to verify."

Jake joined Renard by the navigation chart. He pointed to a circle with an 'X' at its center.

"The *Tai Chiang* is scheduled to meet us there," Jake said, "but it could be anywhere within ten miles of that point. Hell, as fast as that thing moves, it could be anywhere it wants."

Jake opened navigation dividers and measured miles along the length of the chart's side. He drew a ten mile radius around new coordinates.

"My friend is waiting for us there. He'll come when I call him."

"So call him, then," Renard said. "Now would be a good time"

Jake walked to the radio room and lined up the high frequency voice transceiver. Returning to the ship's control panel, he bumped a switch that raised the radio antenna high above the *Colorado*'s sail.

He stepped between the periscopes, twisted dials on the bride-to-bridge radio, and lifted a microphone to his lips.

"Zeus, this is Poseidon, over."

"A bit arrogant," Renard said.

"Shut up!" Jake said and clicked the microphone again. "Zeus, this is Poseidon, over."

Jake stared through the periscope to distract himself from the radio silence that made him uneasy.

In the hazy summer evening sunlight, he saw smoke rise from the engine room and missile compartment hatches that McKenzie had opened. The back of the Trident looked like a pair of smokestacks.

A crackling voice carried excitement.

"Poseidon, this is Zeus, over," Mercer said.

"You're there!" Jake said. "You're a man-god. I'd love to swap stories but we need to be quick. You've got a boat, right?"

"It's a nice rig. I made sixteen knots on the way out here. I have supplies and fuel for at least another week and a half. Over."

"Write this down. I'm thirty-one miles from your rendezvous coordinates, bearing three-two-nine..."

Jake watched Renard, the new GPS fix apparently in his head, trot to the navigation plot and nod affirmation of the coordinates. Jake repeated himself.

"...thirty-one miles, bearing three-two-nine. Did you get that? Over."

"Yeah. Thirty-one miles. Bearing three-two-nine. Over."

"I need you to sprint to me. Max speed. I'll need a ride off this pig soon. Over."

"Consider it done. Zeus, out."

★

Lin watched fog patches roll over the *Tai Chiang's* bow at fifty-one knots. White clouds danced across the bridge windows and yielded only flickering views of blue water.

Kao should have signaled me by now, he thought.

Through breaking mist, his battle control station displayed a passive infrared sweep. A heat plume billowed over the horizon.

"Heat signature of smoke from the direction of the *Colorado,*" he said.

Voices over a loudspeaker caught his attention. It was over a bridge-to-bridge radio frequency, and it was in English between men named Zeus and Poseidon.

You fool, Kao, he thought. *You have been outsmarted by the Americans.*

"The Americans are planning a second rendezvous," he said. "There is damage to the *Colorado* and they have blown to the surface."

"Our stealth is compromised," Yang, the executive officer, said.

"A brilliant analysis, you half-wit. Regardless, we still have hours before even an air asset would find us," Lin said. "We will continue and make haste."

Lin tapped keys on his battle control station that warmed up his ship's remaining four torpedoes and readied its three-inch main gun.

"Man battle stations," he said.

★

"Where's the *Colorado*, sonar room?" Brody asked.

"On the other side of the ice, sir," Schmidt said. "The sound is coming through the hole it made. It blew to the surface and is dead in the water. We just heard its shaft stop."

"How hard will it be for your men to help us fit through the hole the *Colorado* made?" Brody asked.

"It's tight, sir, but we have a lot of noise from the *Colorado* to guide us."

"Tell your guys we're going through."

"Alright, everyone," Brody said. "Listen up. All ahead one-third, make turns for five knots. And let's get our 'A' team up here for depth control. This is going to be tight."

Numbers on digital meters trickled downward as the *Miami* slowed and the ice-roof descended upon it.

"Tripwire," Schmidt said. "Ten feet of ice above the sail."

"Very well, sonar room," Brody said. "Set new tripwire at five feet. Helm, to maneuvering, slow to three knots."

★

Jake watched Renard raise the other periscope.

"I will help you look for the *Tai Chiang*," Renard said.

McKenzie appeared from the ladder. A ring of grime outlined his face.

"Jake, the hatches are open. You can almost see again in the missile compartment, and no sign of the fire reflashing. What next?"

"Go blow the doomsday buoy bolts so we can get to the life rafts. Then drag these canvas survival bags onto the lip around the lower forward escape hatch."

Jake squinted through the optics of the *Colorado*'s number one periscope. Under an early summer Arctic sun, he made out a trace of white water. He twisted the optics to high power to magnify the *Tai Chiang*'s bow-wake. Above the white spray, the black pits of bridge windows encircled the apex of a hazy gray triangle.

"I see the *Tai Chiang*!" he said. "Bearing two-eight-one."

"*Merde*, that ship is stealthy and built for war! Given that he has not shot us, he must still intend to board us."

Jake took his eye off the scope.

"So now what?" he asked.

Renard leaned back and withdrew his Marlboro.

"I will make an offer they cannot resist," Renard said. "Money in exchange for warheads and the fulfillment of my destiny."

CHAPTER THIRTY-TWO

THE AIR HAD CLEARED ENOUGH in the missile compartment so that Jake could read a laminated sheet of instructions through his OBA facemask.

Where's a missile technician when I need one, he thought. *These valve labels are hard to read.*

He twisted an orange hydraulic valve and heard a clunk. A metal ring creaked open above his head, and the missile tube's locking mechanism rotated open.

"Guess that was it," he said.

He awaited word from Renard before twisting the final valve to open the hatch.

In the control room, Renard listened to the commanding officer of the *Tai Chiang* over the radio.

"I will speak only with the Sergeant," Lin said.

"I'm sorry, but he, all of his team, and half of the Americans were killed in a fire," Renard said. "You've seen our smoke?"

"This deviation is unacceptable," Lin said.

"And, I assure you, colliding with a wall of ice and igniting half of this ship were unacceptable deviations as well. We've dealt with them. You, too, must adapt."

"Open the missile hatches."

"Just as soon as you contact your superiors to verify that the final payment has been made."

"Open the hatches!"

Renard watched through the periscope as the *Tai Chiang* came closer.

"Open the hatches, or I will blow them open."

"Shooting at your warheads will only damage them," Renard said. "If you attack us, we will broadcast a message to the United States Coast Guard informing them of our situation. The message is drafted and in our radio queue. We've also inserted the message into two water-activated communications buoys. One buoy is in a launcher, the other is in the arms of the man you see shivering in front of our sail."

"You would threaten me?" Lin asked.

"Not threaten," Renard said. "Warn. This is a lengthy warship. Any weapons you might shoot would be well placed indeed if they're to preclude all means of our informing the Coast Guard."

Renard watched the *Tai Chiang* slow by the *Colorado*'s side.

"I have pulled alongside and will be mating our ships," Lin said. "Open the hatches."

"Soon," Renard said. "I will have Scott return inside the ship with his buoy. While I'm doing that, you will begin the final financial transactions - if you want your warheads."

★

"Tripwire," Schmidt said. "Five feet of ice-"

Brody staggered and grabbed a handrail as the *Miami* dipped and veered. Overhead, metal scraped and ice cracked.

The control room fell silent as the deck leveled.

"Control room, sonar room," Schmidt said, "clear water above. We're free of the icepack."

"Where's the *Colorado*?" Brody asked.

"We hold him on bearing one-nine-two. He's dead in the water, but we have no clue of range. Should we transmit active?" Schmidt asked.

"No, I don't want to alert him. We'll drive the geometry to get his range," Brody said.

"We can have a range in five minutes."

Brody swallowed second thoughts about sealing Jake's fate. Sitting duck or not, he had to die.

"I'm shooting in four minutes," Brody said. "Get me a range in three. Firing point procedures, USS *Colorado*, tube one."

"Mister Renard," Lin said, "I have contacted the appropriate people. Your funds have been transferred. I have been instructed to permit you to verify the monetary transfer. You have wireless phones and know the correct numbers to call. Make haste."

"Splendid! I will open the hatches and verify the funds. If you've lied to me, I will close the hatches on your men's heads."

It is settled, Lin thought. *I am killing that man.*

★

The *Tai Chiang* drifted beside the *Colorado*. A torpedo nest protruded from the stealth craft over the Trident, and a sliding ladder lay on the nest. A Taiwanese sailor lugging a tool bag braved the crawl across the ladder and jumped onto the *Colorado*.

The sailor attacked an inverted cleat with a socket wrench set and rolled it over. Shipmates on the *Tai Chiang* lobbed him a tethered ball. He grabbed it and dragged the attached nylon mooring line to the *Colorado*'s cleat.

The sailor wrapped the line and moved to three more cleats. As shipmates joined him on the Trident, more mooring lines united the vessels.

Missile hatches on the *Colorado*'s port side lay open over the water, offering entrance to the warheads.

★

Brody saw Schmidt's head in a doorway.

"Sir, we have a problem. Some ship just tied up to the *Colorado*. I picked up a fifty-hertz electric plant, but it's a quiet ship. Probably running sound nullifiers on its machinery and masker air around its hull. We only heard it because we were searching in that direction."

"Weapons officer," Brody said. "How much longer until I have to power down the weapon gyros to avoid overheat?"

"Eleven minutes, sir."

"We remain at firing point procedures on the *Colorado*. If there's any sign of counter-detection, we'll shoot," Brody said. "I'm taking the ship to periscope depth to identify the new contact. Raising number two scope."

Through his periscope optics, Brody saw smoke rising from the *Colorado*, but it was the small vessel tied to it that attracted his interest. Its zigzag, hazy gray paint played tricks with his eyes. He also noticed the open missile hatches and men on the deck of the *Colorado*, and the warhead transfer became obvious.

"Executive officer, are we recording the scope optics?" he asked.

"Yes, Captain," Parks said.

"Good, because I have no idea what class of ship that is, but you're not going to believe what they're doing. Can you load this image into a communications buoy?"

"Only a still frame, sir, if you want it done fast and with clarity."

"Then get a still life of this vessel loaded into the primary three-inch launcher. Mark the message for the Chief of Naval Operation's eyes only. Launch it ASAP."

★

After giving him a tongue lashing in front of his crew, Lin had returned Lieutenant Yang to his post as the *Tai Chiang's* executive officer.

Lin listened to him over his headset.

"Simrad acoustic detection," Yang said. "Bearing zero-one-three,"

"Identification!" Lin said.

"Integrators are processing - probable American submarine!"

"This is a trap! Extending starboard torpedo nest."

"Sir," Yang said, "we just received infrared detect on a mast correlating with Simrad detect, range three miles based upon periscope height and Simrad return. The American submarine is shallow."

"Engaging with the cannon," Lin said. "Taking manual gun control."

★

Lowering his OBA breastplate to the control room deck, Jake pulled out his wallet. He dropped it to a desk and withdrew account access codes

"I'm going to pop my head up through the hatch and call my bank, Pierre," he said. "The wireless phones from the *Custom Venture* were global accounts. They should work from here. Let me know when you're ready to make your calls."

"That will settle our finances, but what of our escape? Your friend is not yet here," Renard said.

"Grant should be here in less than an hour, but just in case, keep loading up our sea bags for the life raft."

A crack echoed throughout the control room. Jake peered through the periscope in time to watch the second explosion from the *Tai Chiang's* cannon.

A cubic obelisk spat three-inch shells from a thin barrel in front of the *Tai Chiang's* bridge wing. Every second, the gun popped a round into the sky. Smoke from the end of the barrel wafted over the *Tai Chiang's* bridge.

"What the hell are they shooting at?" Jake asked.

"Not us," Renard said. "That's all that matters at the moment."

★

The flash from the cannon's muzzle gave Brody ten seconds of warning.

"Lowering number two scope," he said. "Helm, all ahead flank. Left five degrees rudder, steady course one-four-zero. Diving officer, make your depth nine-zero feet.

"Weapons officer," he said, "shoot tube one."

Brody's orders hung in the air as the first round from the *Tai Chiang* zipped behind the *Miami*'s sail. The weapon's fused warhead exploded underwater three hundred feet away.

The shockwave shook the *Miami*. Five seconds passed and five more rounds exploded as the *Miami* dived toward the bottom of the hundred-foot sea.

As the ship heeled over, Brody checked a weapons display and verified that his torpedo swam for the *Colorado*.

★

As each pressure wave from the cannon shook the windows of the *Tai Chiang*'s bridge, Lin sited his rounds like an archer adjusting for wind.

His first five shots passed long. As the *Miami*'s periscope slipped underwater, he commanded the ship's combat system to pull back on the gun's distance. The next five rounds were better placed.

The sixth shot grazed the top of the *Miami*'s engine room, rebounding and exploding five feet above. The pressure wave ruptured the *Miami*'s hull and opened a three-foot gash. Water poured in.

The next shot punctured the hull, and its fusing mechanism waited a fraction of a second before detonating the warhead within the *Miami*'s interior. A wall of air, compressed to the density of steel, expanded in the *Miami*'s engine room.

The explosion crumpled heavy panels and baked men in the maneuvering control center into unrecognizable mounds against buckled walls. Flesh vaporized as the blast expanded, and the ocean inundated the *Miami* through the hole ripped in its hull.

CHAPTER THIRTY-THREE

HE OCEAN ERUPTED. WATER WHIPPED turquoise by air and bioluminescence sprayed toward the sky.

"They're shooting at a sub!" Jake said. "Shit! It's probably the *Miami*. It's emergency surfacing."

"Your friend has found us, but the *Tai Chiang* has found him," Renard said.

Jake forgot about his personal battles and walked to switches that controlled the *Colorado's* ballast tank vents.

"What are you doing?" Renard asked.

"Submerging to drag the *Tai Chiang* under with us."

"We have no time to shut the hatches!"

"They're sitting ducks," Jake said. "I can't let this happen. I have to do something."

"Did you not hear me?" Renard asked. "The hatches are open! You're not submerging, you're sinking our ship!"

Jake flipped switches and opened the vents to the *Colorado's* ballast tanks.

"This ship's already a tomb," he said.

Renard blew smoke from the corner of his mouth.

"Very well," Renard said. "You've made your decision, and the clock is ticking, *mon ami*. You have a plan?"

"Put a jacket on and grab a shotgun," Jake said. "Follow me out the forward hatch. We've got a life raft to open. 'Plan B' is now in effect."

"'Plan B' - designed in the case that your friend did not arrive – assumes that we evade on a life raft. Correct?" Renard asked.

"Yes," Jake said.

"But does it consider that the *Tai Chiang* might be hostile?"

"The *Tai Chiang* is going to be tied to the *Colorado* and underwater in ten minutes. If not, that's what the shotguns and rifles are for."

The tug at Jake's sleeve marked the first time Renard had volunteered to touch him. The Frenchman's knuckles were white, and Jake saw fear in his face.

"Jake," Renard said, "I disapprove of 'Plan B'."

"You've got a better idea?"

Renard released Jake's sleeve.

"No," he said. "I can only pray that you're still charmed."

Jake yanked a parka from McKenzie's hands and put it on. It smelled stale and felt heavy and warm. He climbed a ladder through the lower of two hatches. Crouched over the lower hatch, he braced his footing and reached for the upper, twisted it open, and salty air chilled his face.

"Scott, hand me that rifle and get these sea bags topside. Pierre, follow me up with a shotgun."

Jake lifted himself through the hatch and felt the Arctic cold envelop him. He whispered to Renard as his silvery head emerged.

"Give me your shotgun."

"Are we going to kill them?" Renard asked.

"I don't know."

Shivering under his parka, Jake skirted the sail as the *Tai Chiang*'s gun muzzle repositioned for another volley half a football field away. The *Colorado* had already slipped two feet into the ocean and was pulling the *Tai Chiang* over.

As Jake rounded the back of the sail, four Taiwanese sailors working in an opened hatch came into view. Two of them held a canvas cloth that bulged with the weight of a conical warhead. Beyond them, three missile hatches dangled above the water on their massive hinges.

Jake pointed an M-16 rifle at the men, whistled, and pointed to the deck. The sailors lowered the warhead. Jake then pointed toward the *Tai Chiang* and returned his hand back to the barrel stock.

The men darted down the *Colorado*'s back. Two more men jumped from the missile hatch, dropped their tools, and sprinted after their comrades.

Jake knelt by the forward doomsday buoy nest. Renard helped him shove a metal covering aside.

"Hurry! The water's rising," Jake said.

McKenzie dropped a canvas bag by Jake's feet and helped the other two men pluck the yellow life raft from the nest.

"Stand back!" Jake said.

He yanked a cord. Compressed air hissed, and the raft unfolded. Two plastic paddles lay strapped in the center.

"Detach the cover, grab your weapons and those sea bags, and get in," Jake said. "The water will come to us. Be ready to paddle away so we don't get sucked under."

★

The eighth through tenth rounds from the *Tai Chiang's* gun missed. Lin realized that he was shooting behind the submarine and ceased fire. He tapped the battle control station. The gun swiveled, and Lin awaited input from infrared sensors that would paint the submarine better than his naked eye.

He gazed through the bridge window and saw smoke rising from a hole in the *Miami*, then glanced at his infrared display. Shining white light highlighted the wounds ripped in the *Miami*'s engine room.

He tapped the battle control station and watched the cannon barrel steady. Three shots rang out at the surfaced submarine but landed short. Lin scanned the infrared of the *Miami* again and instructed the gun to shoot a degree higher.

A voice crackled in his headset.

"Sir," Yang said, "the ship has a four degree list."

"Adjusting the cannon!" Lin said.

The barrel of the weapon recoiled three more times. Smoke blew by the windows.

"Sir, the list is now six degrees," Yang said. "The weapon is missing because of the list."

A lookout from the port bridge wing popped his head through a door.

"Captain, the work team has been forced at gunpoint to abandon the missile load."

Lin saw Jake and his men boarding an inflatable raft, his work team sprinting across the deck, and the waterline creeping up to the *Colorado*'s missile deck.

"We're being pulled under," he said. "All hands lay to the cleats. Cast off all lines!"

Lin watched the *Colorado*'s engine room and missile compartment hatches swallow the sea. A whirlpool swept one of his sailors down the missile compartment hatch.

Men on his bridge wing balanced against a list that had accelerated past thirty-degrees. They tried to untie the line, but with the line under tension and the cleats in the frigid sea, they could not. One by one, they plunged into the water.

On the *Tai Chiang's* bow, a team of sailors fell into the sea with a flailing line snaking behind them.

At least one group of these imbeciles understands line handling, Lin thought.

The ocean had swallowed all but the *Colorado*'s conning tower sail as three mooring lines dragged Lin under. The *Tai Chiang* creaked around him as water pushed against its watertight windows. He thought about trying to escape through the starboard door above.

As he reached for his seat straps, he heard a nylon line snap. Another line popped, and the bow swiveled.

Counting on the last line to yield under the strain, Lin smirked, began programming a torpedo to attack the *Miami*, and waited.

★

Jake paddled with all his strength. McKenzie grunted beside him as Renard glued binoculars to his face.

"What do you see?" Jake asked.

"The *Colorado* is almost gone, and the *Tai Chiang* is ninety degrees over, but the lines are snapping."

"Fine," Jake said. "Let them come for us. Reach into those bags and break out the rifles."

★

In passive mode, the *Miami*'s torpedo sought the loudest mechanical noises in the ocean - the rhythmic harmonies of the *Colorado*'s dying reactor plant.

Frigid streams flowed through the mechanical forest of the engine room. Water had risen to the compartment's middle level, but fluid still flowed through pipes, and pumps continued to rotate. The *Colorado*'s reactor plant churned out the sustaining power it needed in its waning moments to keep itself alive.

Salt water seeped into electrical circuits. Breakers popped open and the ship turned dark. Reactor circuitry de-energized, causing control rod drive mechanisms to release the neutron absorbent rods into the core.

Within the confines of the dry, watertight reactor compartment, the *Colorado*'s core shut itself down.

Homing in on the sounds of the *Colorado*'s dying reactor plant, the *Miami*'s torpedo detonated above the submarine's hull.

The ADCAP torpedo vaporized the steel above the Trident's engine room. The compressed energy of the heavyweight torpedo expanded into the engine room, vaporized metal, and sent the *Colorado* to the ocean floor.

★

Lin held the battle control station for support and listened for the last mooring line to snap. He never heard that sound, nor did he hear the ADCAP explode fifty feet behind his head.

The torpedo's blast transformed water into a superheated gas, and its energy vaporized the *Tai Chiang*'s hull. The shock wave compressed steam to the density of steel, pounded the interior of the small warship, and pulverized Lin.

The scattered molecules of DNA evidence of Lin's existence settled with the warped and gutted hull of the *Tai Chiang* on the sea floor.

CHAPTER THIRTY-FOUR

B RODY SCANNED THE HORIZON THROUGH the periscope. The ocean had swallowed all evidence of the *Colorado* and the *Tai Chiang*, but a bright orange blob caught his eye. He switched to high power and settled his gaze on tiny forms in a life raft.

Brody doubted he would understand what had compelled his protégé to steal the *Colorado*, but he would never have another chance to thank Jake for saving him from the phantom warship. Trusting that fate would administer whatever justice Jake deserved, Brody allowed the man who had saved his life twice to escape.

"Should I raise the other periscope to help you look for contacts, sir?" Parks asked.

"No," Brody said. "There's nothing out there, and there's nothing we could do about it if there were. This ship's entire crew should be committed to damage control, restoring propulsion, and caring for the injured."

"We're doing all we can, sir," Parks said. "I've seen to it. But don't you think we should look for survivors?"

Brody sighed.

"Any man who survived our torpedo – and that's a big 'if' - is freezing to death in the water right now. We're three miles away, and we can only make three knots. No man could possibly survive an hour in this sea. Turning back would be useless, and since our pumps aren't keeping pace back aft, we need to head to shore to save our ship."

★

Jake shivered, but dry clothes and parkas kept him and his two companions alive. He raised a bridge-to-bridge radio to his mouth.

"Cut your engines," he said. "You're close enough. We'll paddle from here."

In his trawler's pilothouse, Mercer raised his thumb.

Jake lowered the radio, grabbed a paddle, and leaned over the lip of the raft. He dipped the paddle into the water.

"Row hard Scotty. We might not be alone out here much longer."

Jake felt his back cramping, but he kept paddling until the raft bumped into fiberglass. A rope ladder landed by his knees. He climbed two rungs and accepted Mercer's hand.

"Thanks, buddy," he said.

Jake hugged his friend.

"You smell worse than my ass," Jake said.

"Blame yourself. It's a pain to shower in this thing, and you're six days late," Mercer said.

"We ran into some trouble."

Jake reached over the trawler's side and helped his companions up.

"This is Pierre," he said. "And this is Scotty."

"I was expecting four guys," Mercer said.

"Lost two. Gained one. Long story," Jake said.

"I hate to ruin the reunion," Renard said, "but we still need to check our accounts to ensure that we've been paid. We will need to shift the codes before Taiwan learns of the *Tai Chiang's* fate."

"Go ahead," Jake said.

Renard placed a wireless phone to his cheek. He spoke in French, but Jake didn't need to translate it. The inflexion in the Frenchman's voice and the smile that spread across his face told him that each man in the trawler was much richer than he had been the day before.

★

In the Oval Office, President Ryder studied a picture of the *Tai Chiang*. He inhaled through his bulbous nose.

"And you say this was a Taiwanese vessel, Admiral?"

"That's correct, Mister President," Mesher said.

"Taiwan tried to steal our warheads?"

"Yes, sir. We were right about the intent but assumed the wrong assailants when we focused on the Middle East."

"The Prime Minister's got some explaining to do, but I'll have someone take that up with the unofficial ambassador. I want you to tell me how we're cleaning up this mess. How's the *Miami*?"

"Sir, the *Miami* made its way to a Coast Guard base in western Alaska. We flew in a welding team to place cover plates on its hull. We're going to tow the *Miami* to Bangor, Washington, for dry-dock repairs. She'll be out of commission for a year."

"What about the crew?"

"Nine died in the attack."

Ryder remembered comrades lost during Vietnam.

"This country owes them a debt."

"We can't publicize their heroism, sir," Mesher said, "but we'll honor them and compensate their survivors as we do with covert operations casualties."

"How about the injured?"

"The rest of the crew escaped without major injury. The damage was contained to the engine room. We'll need a crew aboard that ship for safety and security, but I've authorized the *Miami* to fly half of its crew home to Groton for a few weeks. Then they'll rotate with the other half before they take the submarine south."

"Good decision. All those men are heroes."

"Yes, sir. They are."

"What about awards? Promotions? That crew showed character. The skipper had guts."

"Plenty of accolades, sir. And the captain, John Brody – turns out he knew Slate. Slate actually saved his life a few years ago."

Ryder reflected upon the irony of Slate having saved Brody's life so that he could later deliver his death blow.

"So Brody swallowed his feelings and did his job," Ryder said. "We need more men like him in command."

"Agreed, sir."

"What about the *Colorado?*" Ryder asked.

"We're anchoring an oceanographic research vessel on top of her. The water is shallow enough that we can use divers to retrieve the warheads."

"Then what? If the public discovers that a Trident submarine is lying in a hundred feet of water thirty-five miles from the Russian coast, there's going to be hell to pay. I said that thing was destroyed in the Atlantic for Christ's sake!" Ryder said.

"After we remove the warheads, we'll remove the missiles and dismantle them in guarded secrecy. We'll repeat the process with the torpedoes. The reactor core will be moved and carted piece by piece to Idaho for burial. It'll take the remainder of the summer."

"There will still be a huge chunk of a Trident's carcass on the ocean floor."

"We'll snap its hull into smaller pieces and dispose of them."

"Won't there be scattered evidence on the sea bed?" Ryder asked.

"Yes, sir, and it'll take until after next winter's thaw to clean. But this took place in the middle of nowhere, and we'll be guarding the site."

Ryder stood and stared out the window at the White House lawn. He began to believe that his legacy could survive the *Colorado* Incident.

"How soon until the bodies of Slate and his accomplices can be recovered and verified?"

"Sir, an ADCAP torpedo can vaporize metal. I can't promise you a body."

"I feared as much, but he's not the only guilty one in this. What are we doing to those bastards who gave Slate HIV and covered it up?"

"The investigation revealed that Commander Thomas Henry knowingly transferred HIV to Slate. It took some bold men to step forward and admit to homosexuality and risk their careers, but with their help, we got to the truth."

Ryder grunted.

"I dislike how we treat gays in the military. Brave witnesses just gave up their careers to support a system that doesn't support them."

"Not necessarily," Mesher said. "There's a little known clause about homosexuality and military service."

"Oh?"

"A serviceman may experiment with homosexuality, but unless he admits to being, or is proven to be, a practicing homosexual, there's no need for administrative action."

"So to make the case against Commander Henry, you're going to have witnesses say that they were just experimenting?"

"No, sir. We won't ask and they won't tell."

"Well put," Ryder said.

"As for Henry, given that his charges include physical assault against an officer by knowingly giving Slate HIV, I've had him thrown in the brig. The senior officers who tried to cover up what Henry did to Slate are awaiting Courts Martial, too."

Ryder crossed his arms and shook his head.

"A cover up involving a flag officer. Why?"

"Henry was the strongest candidate to replace the only black submarine admiral. They thought they were protecting the needs of the service by protecting Henry."

"This mess is still ugly, but it looks like you're covered on all fronts. I was damned anxious for a while."

"I was too, sir," Mesher said.

"You should have been. Your job was on the line."

"I'm retiring in nine months," Mesher said. "Thanks to Commander John Brody, I won't have to retire nine months early."

Ryder returned to his desk and sat.

"I'd almost forgotten," Ryder said. "I assume I'm still invited to your farewell ceremony?"

"Of course, sir."

"Any plans to add to your legacy – other than burying the details of the *Colorado* Incident so deeply that it would take a team of archeologists to unearth?"

"Just one, sir. I'm adding a submarine captain to the short list of people I want to make admiral."

"Commander Brody?" Ryder asked.

"No, sir. Captain Brody, as of tonight."

★

Wearing jeans and a sweatshirt, Brody took a limousine shuttle from Bradley International Airport to his home in Groton, Connecticut.

He tried to forget the faces of the crewmen he had lost. Although Pete Parks would tend to the *Miami* during his absence, he would always consider the *Miami* his.

He trotted toward the house, and hope burst through his chest as he noticed the flickering of a television. He fumbled with his house key and rushed through the door.

"Carole?" he asked.

He continued to the living room. On the couch, his wife slept. He knelt by her side.

She awoke and her eyes sparkled.

"John?"

"Yeah, honey. It's me."

"I was afraid you were dead," she said. "After you were late coming back, they told us not to worry, but the thought of never having you back scared me."

"That's how I felt about you. I'm ready to do it right this time. I've stopped drinking. It feels good to have my head clear. I won't start again."

"I know you can do it. You're a strong man, and you're the best commanding officer in the fleet as far as I'm concerned. I don't care if you ever make admiral."

"That's good honey, because after what I did I'm lucky if they don't bust me to seaman."

Carole rolled off the couch and walked across the room to a small carton resting on the television. Watching her move reminded him of their honeymoon so many years earlier.

"What are you doing?" he asked.

She pulled a full-bird captain's hat out of the box.

"Your commodore called me yesterday," she said. "He let me use this as a little ice-breaker. The order came from the CNO himself. You're officially 'Captain Brody'."

She put the hat on his head.

"I'd still love you if you were a seaman," she said, "but that does look good."

Brody kissed his wife.

★

Wind whipping his face, Jake drew a fur-lined parka hood over his head. Even in June, the wind blowing across the Bering Strait reddened his skin.

He kicked a pebble. He had killed too many men to have placed warheads on the ocean floor, and his plan for vengeance had missed its goal. But he could now see that his anger had driven him to the edge of destruction.

Beside him, Mercer and McKenzie battled two toddlers to a staring match stalemate. Renard approached and placed his hand on one of the children's pelt-covered heads.

"My Russian is crude," the Frenchman said, "but I believe that I just traded our trawler for an automobile."

Jake looked over a wooden dock at the trawler that had plucked him from a life raft. A trout fisherman, adorned in furs like his two children, climbed into the boat.

"Not that I hoped to keep it," Mercer said, "but you just traded my trawler for peanuts."

"I would prefer to take my chances driving through a barren land than chancing an ocean trip to Vladivostok," Renard said.

"What then?" Jake asked.

"No one knows I was involved, no one who would speak of it anyway. We can hide in Vladivostok while we await your new French passports from my assistant."

"Passports?" Jake asked.

"With new identities," Renard said. "God willing, you're all taken for dead by any nation that would care. For simplicity of travel, I'm reinventing you as Frenchmen."

A breeze caught Jake on the neck, and he coughed.

"Ah," Renard said. "That reminds me. I should arrange for medical care upon our return. I imagine that it has been a while since you've measured your blood count."

"I feel fine," Jake said.

"Really? I feel horrible. When I get to Lyon, I will sleep for a week."

"I'm tired, too, but I think the worst thing is that I don't know what to do next," Jake said.

"*C'est la vie,*" Renard said. "You must live it day by day."

Renard removed his gloves, tucked them in his pockets, and flipped the gold-plated Zippo under a Marlboro. He smiled as he exhaled smoke, but Jake couldn't force himself to return the gesture.

"You still appear bothered," Renard said.

"We came up short," Jake said. "We didn't get the warheads to Taiwan."

"Taiwanese sailors had a warhead in their possession, did they not?" Renard asked.

"Yeah."

"Then the way I see it, we accomplished our mission but changed our minds for the sake of the *Miami*. Accomplishments mean nothing if you sacrifice your humanity. Fortunately, we did not have to," Renard said, "and we still were well compensated for our efforts."

He smiled.

"Well, I'm HIV positive, I don't have a home, and the only people in my life are standing here. And Mercer is taking McKenzie with him to Spain before McKenzie moves on to South America."

"It's best that our little group is not seen together, at least for several years," Renard said.

"So how many friends does that leave me?"

"One. You will be safe with me in Lyon. You can perfect your French and buy the best medical care."

"What makes you think I want to perfect my French?"

"For the lovely French women waiting for you in Lyon, of course."

"Women who want to get HIV?"

"No, *mon ami*. You're not the first to suffer from the condition. I asked my fiancée to locate social and support groups in the city. You're not alone in this world."

"You've looked out for me from the beginning," Jake said. "I don't know what to say except 'thanks'."

"I told you three oceans ago. I'm genuinely concerned about you."

Renard blew a cloud that floated over the head of an approaching fisherman. He leaned toward the fisherman and exchanged words in Russian. The man patted Renard on the back, smiled, and walked away.

"The deal is closed," Renard said. "We have a car."

"Okay," Jake said. "But what's this talk about a fiancée? You never said you were getting married."

"Marie was not my fiancée until an hour ago."

"Marie? That's who you're in love with? I forgot all about her. If it wasn't for her, we never would've met."

Renard flicked the butt of a Marlboro into the river and smiled again.

"She did make our meeting possible, but I believe that I have ample place in my heart to forgive her."

THE END

ABOUT THE AUTHOR

JOHN HINDINGER GRADUATED FROM THE U.S. Naval Academy in 1991 and served aboard the USS *Kentucky*, a Trident Missile submarine, prior to becoming a top-rated instructor of American submarine and international naval combat tactics at the U.S. Naval Submarine School.

He earned a Master of Science degree in Electrical Engineering from Rensselaer, an MBA from the University of Chicago, and a Professional Engineer's License. After four years in Ford Motor Company's Information Technology department, he founded Jade Biomed, a company that develops alternative medical equipment.

Printed in the United Kingdom by
Lightning Source UK Ltd., Milton Keynes
137078UK00002B/114/A